THE

STOCKHOLM

SYNDROME

PRESIDENT

HOW TRUMP TRIGGERED OBAMA'S
HIDDEN CONFESSION

Andrew G. Hodges, M.D.

Author Website: www.andrewghodges.com

Village House Publishers
Birmingham, AL

PUBLISHED IN THE UNITED STATES OF AMERICA

Regarding *Thoughtprint Decoding*

As a former district attorney, I am convinced that Dr. Hodges makes a compelling case for 'thoughtprints' in solving criminal cases and their potential for forensic evaluations. Practicing as a trial lawyer for years in the county in California where a judge first allowed DNA to be admitted into evidence, I am particularly attune to innovative new methods of forensic investigation. Recently, our branch of the national educational legal society (Inns of Court) consisting of eighty lawyer/ judge members featured the 'thoughtprint decoding' method as the central presentation.

Richard A. Regnier, Attorney
Diplomate National Board of Trial Advocacy

Having investigated criminal matters for 26 years, I find that Dr. Hodges' study of the deeper intelligence is a real breakthrough in criminal investigations. I wish I had known about his method while I was still conducting investigations.

Charles Donald Byron
Special Agent, FBI (retired)

Indeed a new type of investigator is on the forensic scene. The discovery of the super intelligence is like the discovery of DNA. Hodges' profiling method offers us hidden confessions and chilling explanations as to motives when forensic documents or oral interrogations are available.

(the late) Irving Weisberg, Ph.D., psychologist
Faculty member, Adelphi University
Garden City, New York

Dr. Hodges has successfully applied a sound and validated method of decoding the unconscious mind to the world of criminal investigation. This exciting work demands serious consideration.

M. Mark McKee, Psy.D.
Associate Professor of Psychology
Illinois School of Professional Psychology

In his book on the Natalee Holloway case, Dr. Hodges steps 'out of the box' of conventional law enforcement forensic techniques and shares a remarkable method that reveals one's truth – truth that is thought to be safely locked away. What a powerful tool – law enforcement should wrap their arms around this!

Janice Windham
Supervisory Special Agent, FBI (retired)

Dr. Hodges advances forensic psychiatry and forensic profiling—both lacking new tools particularly in solving puzzling cases. With "thoughtprint decoding" Hodges offers a solid way of getting at crucial overlooked clues. Based on clinical and mathematical work, "thoughtprints" is completely consistent with the notion that every criminal leaves behind clues about their crime. In this gem, Hodges deals with little known workings of the mind that reveal vital information in a disguised form. For the reader who wants the best look imaginable at the criminal mind, this will be a fascinating read.

Harold S. Schaus, Jr., M.S., DAPA Past President
The Society for Communicative Psychoanalysis and Psychotherapy

To the millions of Americans who believe
none of us is above the rule of law,
not even a president.

Also from Andrew G. Hodges

Jesus: An Interview Across Time
(A Psychiatrist Looks at His Humanity)

The Deeper Intelligence
(The Breakthrough to the Untapped Potential of Your Subconscious Mind)

A Mother Gone Bad
(The Hidden Confession of JonBenet's Killer)

Who Will Speak for JonBenet?
(A New Investigator Reads Between the Lines)

Into The Deep
(The Hidden Confession of Natalee's Killer)

The Obama Confession
(Secret Fear, Secret Fury)

Behind Nazi Lines
(My Father's Heroic Quest to Save 149 WW II POWs)
with Denise George

As Done Unto You
(The Secret Confession of Amanda Knox)

ANDREW G. HODGES, M.D., is a psychiatrist in private practice, a former clinical professor of psychiatry (UAB School of Medicine), and a noted forensic profiler. Experts including experienced FBI agents believe his unique "thoughtprint decoding" method will one day become a fixture in law enforcement much as identifying fingerprints. The author of nine books, Dr. Hodges has been interviewed on Fox News, CNN, ABC, MSNBC and Court TV.

TABLE OF CONTENTS

Introduction

A Mole in the White House

Barrack Obama is playing the highest stakes game of political poker, betting against the truth as he raises the stakes against the world. In the process, he has put the very existence of America and the entire globe on the table by shifting the balance of power toward radical Islam. And he has no conscious idea he's doing it.

The story is closely tied to the presidential election of 2016 and beyond.

Even the best of professional poker players have "poker tells"—unconscious clues including body language that secretly tip their hand. Their opponents must remain constantly on the lookout for such tells.

In the same way Obama has secret tells that reveal the powerful but frightening hand he's holding.

If you want to see that hand clearly, there's only one way to do it. *You have to know how he communicates unconsciously.*

This is what I do—read secret tells in political leaders just as I have done as a forensic psychiatrist profiling criminal cases of guilty perpetrators.

To jump ahead briefly, we will find that Donald Trump astutely reads Obama more accurately than almost anyone else. Given his own high-stakes investment background, Donald Trump both consciously and unconsciously has picked up on key Obama "tells" far beyond what even he appreciates. Trump is part of the story Obama secretly unfolds.

Decoding explained

Obama reveals major tells in a two key speeches he made in June. Understand we're in a new day and age about decoding unconscious communication. Only recently have we learned how to read subconscious messages.

We've discovered an unconscious super intelligence that *quick-reads* every situation in the blink of an eye with phenomenal accuracy far more perceptive than our conscious minds.

The super-intel then communicates verbally. It quick-reads and quick-speaks. It tells—what it sees. *Verbal tells.* When you read those verbal tells, you hear the deeper mind speaking. That's how it gives up its darkest secrets.

The great verbal tell is that the conscious mind speaks literally while the unconscious mind speaks symbolically—in essence in code.

It's amazingly basic. While the conscious mind describes literal events, the super-intel speaks symbolically—figuratively—weaving a secret story together with matching symbolic images.

Learning to read Obama's messages symbolically rather than literally is the first major step toward decoding his tells.

Obama's super-intel is constantly quick reading him—and operates on a deeper moral compass that must tell the truth the conscious mind overlooks or conceals. It does so in three *basic psycholinguistic codes.* First in "protesting too much" denials: "I'm not this, not doing this." Read through the denial to hear, "I *am* doing this." Most commonly the super-intel speaks in "log in the eye" projections using powerful symbolic imagery. In other words when someone telling you something about someone else, it's secretly about himself. Look for matching symbolic imagery that tells a cohesive story.

I have called these matching symbolic messages "thoughtprints" which you can track for consistent messages—like mental fingerprints. As an investigator I'm always asking if the denials, the projections and the imagery match—and together tell a powerful story. My forensic profiling method is called "thoughtprint decoding."

Above all the super-intel is a secret story-teller. And Obama tells one powerful convincing story. His brilliant super-intel takes us to his deepest motivations in the whisk of a broom.

Obama's secret story

Here's the story Obama tells in code. He's severely abusing America and can't see it. He thinks his ideology is correct. Consciously he's in massive denial, but his super-intel tells us the unbelievable truth about him, a truth even his greatest critics don't know.

Secretly he's a controlled mole in the White House and has no idea. He tells us how it came to be, by identifying the disturbing baggage he brought to the White House.

It seems impossible an idealized president has such baggage, so heavy he can't pick it up, can't look at it consciously. But consider his consistently harmful decisions.

The world's closing in on America. There are multiple global "hot spots' with no one minding the store.

A quick tour of his national security policies reveals ISIS unchecked and growing in power—its terrorists immigrating to America. The Middle East is in chaos except for Iran which is advancing and taking aim at Israel for a nuclear attack in five years or less. Will America follow? If you doubt it, remember that Iranian patrol boats have recently been harassing U.S. Navy warships in the Gulf, a sign of aggression which no prior American president would have tolerated.

Russia continues to freely assert its will and expand its borders. Vladimir Putin has already conquered Crimea, a part of Ukraine—and threatens to use well-equipped armor divisions to take over Ukraine in its entirety.

China is asserting its will by building artificial islands with landfills on existing reefs in the ocean—on which they plan to construct military airstrips to threaten the South Pacific including Hawaii and the Philippines. They want regional domination over the United States—and Obama says nothing.

North Korea's maniacal dictator, Kim Jong-un, continues developing ICBMs—testing them monthly—until eventually they can reach the U.S. mainland. Japan's harbors serious concerns that neither Obama nor Hillary would defend any Korean aggression toward them.

All these aggressive nations know that Obama's weak and offers no meaningful response except empty words. All the while he cancels plans for the missile defense shield in Eastern Europe, weakens our armed forces including the officer corps, and fails to protect our borders inviting more Syrian Muslims into the country—terrorists unquestionably among them.

Within our borders Obama continues to attack the rule of law with executive orders, supports gun-control in order to rob citizen's right to self-defense and undermines law enforcement—ever true to his training of disrupting our society, training he received at the feet of America-haters such as Saul Alinsky, Bill Ayers and Jeremiah Wright Jr. Frighteningly, Obama is simply not who he says or thinks he is.

He has created a cancer in our society which urgently must be addressed—or we sanction his ongoing abuse. Be sure Hillary Clinton has the same plan. She represents the cancer metastasized.

Hillary's baggage

Clinton brings her own two tons of baggage to her potential presidency. She's already shown her anti-American colors.

As Secretary of State, she allowed the Benghazi embassy attacks to occur with Obama himself unavailable but, as usual, never held accountable. Hillary failed to protect U.S. Ambassador Christopher Stevens in Libya who died in a 2012 terrorist attack on the anniversary of 9/11 no less. She ignored his repeated requests for protection claiming in a lie she didn't know about those desperate requests. Immediately she doubled down deceitfully, telling everyone that an American video led to the attack—another bald-faced lie she has never owned. Obama totally had her back as he danced to the cover-up music endorsing the lie for weeks, once again escaping any accountability for his deceit.

Hillary Clinton continually demonstrated her own unique skills for creating chaos throughout the Middle East, encouraging the removal of Libya's stable leader. All the while she's bowing and scraping to Russia in her own magnificent "reset" button of the relationship. In actuality she reset America's national security to a major downgrade.

Likewise she enabled ISIS's continued rise with barely a peep, seconding every motion Obama's made on how to unwisely handle matters. Under a Clinton administration we can expect much of the same Obama foreign policy of turning the other cheek.

Also, as Secretary of State she in effect posted America's security protections and secret issues all over the Internet with her multiple unsecured electronic devices. She failed to do her most basic job to protect America. Casting her judgment to the wind, she had her own special need called "Look after Hillary—and the money coming in" for the Clinton Foundation. Her byword, "Leaders of the world, show me my money." Then she pleads, "I forgot" as in "I never knew

5

Secretary of State privileged communications were classified.

One job failure after another. We can only imagine how proud community organizer/disrupter and saboteur supreme Saul Alinsky would have been of his former pupil. Dating back to the publication of his 1971 treatise, *Rules for Radicals,* Alinsky became a popular guru of America's racial and left-wing agitators. Alinsky boldly dedicated *Rules for Radicals* to "Lucifer."

From Hillary's extensive Wellesley College thesis on Alinsky in 1969 to ongoing personal contact, it's clear that he significantly influenced her primary strategy on encouraging "victims" to organize in the name of freedom. It spilled over to her own entitlement needs as a victim and the freedom to take as much make-up money and power as she needed. It was never enough.

Hillary has continually tried to minimize Alinsky's substantial influence on her, but it's clear that she shares Obama's admiration for the Alinsky model: destroy American from within.

Madame Hillary has a self-sabotaging streak a mile wide and will take America with her.

She's now standing at the border waving in the illegal immigrants, inviting legions of "legal" Syrian immigrants some of whom are terrorists. Iran's on the move, and Hillary's plans to fuel their planes. She's addicted to money, and her administration would continue to be addicted to taxpayers' money.

Hillary's severe abuse
As a significant abuse victim, Hillary Rodham Clinton has a longstanding history of suffering spousal emotional abuse in the form of husband Bill's obsessive infidelities which continue to this day. While she consciously accepts her abuse, unconsciously she's understandably paranoid and easily enraged. A recent book by a former Secret Service agent

documents her seething, barely secret rage[1] confirmed by multiple other sources. The general public has just an inkling of the pain with which she lives.

Already she demonstrates the classic signs of a severe abuse victim who's programmed to take out her rage on others. Step back. All her Secretary of State behavior— exposing America's own security to great danger, destruction of the Middle East's stability, enabling Russia and Iran's increased powers, constantly lying and flaunting her right to do so, her vast entitlement to all the money she can get her hands on, and finally costing the lives of Christopher Stevens along with several soldiers—reflects the rage of a woman gone almost mad.

As sure as the sun rises, Hillary's abuse of America will worsen day by day. She's fixated in her payback role, only now she can attack as never before. Understand America and the White House symbolize in one grand unconscious plan her betrayer-in-chief, Bill Clinton, who has brought down unimaginable shame upon her in such a devil-may-care public fashion.

As president, she would now be free to attack, to retaliate like never before—to totally destroy her beloved abuser, Bill, by destroying America. In the end punishing herself at her own hands.

Already we hear the word on the street, "Hillary's going to be worse than Obama." She's got the programming to do it. In certain ways, she matches Obama's personal trauma but then again as he tells us the severity of his early programming is off the charts.

Eight more years of presidential abuse?

In any case, the pattern points inexorably to eight more years of leader abuse.

Are we there yet? Are Obama and Clinton supporters so

---

[1] Crisis of Character, Gary J. Bryne, Center Street, New York, June, 2016

caught up in the kick-me role that they simply can't protect themselves? It's certainly in us as human beings to easily get caught up in such a dynamic. History shouts that fact at us. The citizens of great nations tend to allow abuse by their leaders until it all falls down on everybody. It happens over and over again.

But at this propitious moment, we the people of America and the world are playing with a new fire. The proliferation of nuclear weapons increase the probability of nuclear war, and there are mad men out there set on the loose by Obama especially, soon followed by Hillary Clinton if she captains America's ship, to oblige every one and carry out the final dirty deed. One person who saw the frightening potential in human nature was Albert Einstein.

Now we see all the destructive finished business that can occur from the massive baggage of "unfinished business" that Obama and Hillary both carry with them buried below the surface of their damaged psyches. It can finish the world off— or a lot more of it than we could ever conceive in our wildest dreams.

That's the potential power of unconscious programming and disguised unbridled rage carried out with the cover-up of a smile on both their faces. Believe it.

We are looking potentially at two unconscious moles in the White House who do not have America's interest at heart. With their defective moral compass leading them to place themselves above the law, they both remain in complete denial of the rule of law delivered to us by our founders. We would then have the first female abusive president on the heels of Obama's abuse.

But deep down in his soul, Barack Obama's super-intel tries to come to our rescue. He sees the nightmare Hillary would be—a clone of himself as a prisoner to her programming—and unconsciously he wants to set them both free, and set America free. That's why he will secretly tell us he knows Trump should be president. *That's why he tells us the story of his secret programming even though he's never consciously faced it.*

Obama has a wife and kids and grasps deep down that he's putting everyone at risk including his own family. He delivers a passionate plea for all Americans.

The author's connection to this election

I have a personal connection to the White House and this election. In 1994, then esteemed U.S. Senate Chaplain Richard Halverson personally took my book *The Deeper Intelligence* to then-President Bill Clinton and his First Lady, Hillary Clinton. Halverson had been a longstanding Washington, D.C. pastor before becoming Senate chaplain and was venerated by our nation's leaders. About my book he said, "It's as if God planned this crucial book for this moment in time. Secularism, having ravaged our culture is now exhausted."

Understand it was the idea he grasped as crucial that we have an unconscious super intelligent moral compass entirely separate from our conscious mind compass. A deeper natural law moral compass exactly as our founders insisted that operated on "the laws of nature and Nature's God." The laws of life, liberty and the pursuit of happiness. Dr. Halverson had seen our leaders dramatically drift away from our basic foundation.

Of course, the Clintons had no use for the idea that they were accountable to a deeper moral compass—that they were not above the rule of law. They were both too abused and too abusive to consider it.

Obama's in a similar boat, but his programming is deeper and more complete than Hillary's. Yet at the same time his super-intel desperately longs to be true to his deeper moral compass for an intensely personal reason. Deep down, he also knows that we're on a precipice—as so many sense today.

He wants a different legacy than the one he has forged

with his destructive, pro-Islam policies. This why he pleads with America to see who he really is and stop him—and his plans to continue his abuse of America. Don't think he's going away. He has set America on a downhill course and aims to continue its slide.

Who can hear him? Only those who have developed their super-intel ears, tuning into deeper messages.

1

TRUMP TRIGGERS OBAMA CONFESSION

Following the worst mass murder in U.S. history in which 49 people were killed and 53 wounded on June 12, 2016, at a nightclub in Orlando, Fla., Barack Hussein Obama delivered two back-to-back speeches on June 12 and 14, revealing who he really is. It's the greatest secret story in America.

Soon he will inform us that the very future of America rides on how well we understand this story.

Having been pressured by more than seven years of failed national security policies, Obama was specifically triggered by Donald Trump who tweeted that Obama "disgracefully refused to say the words, 'radical Islam,'" and called for Obama to "step down" immediately. The next day Trump added that Obama was either totally ignorant ("doesn't get it") or something more sinister was transpiring. It was possible, Trump concluded, that Obama "gets it better than anyone understands" implying the president's personal responsibility for the attack. The mainstream media castigated Trump over the tweets, but he was spot on.

Trump's deeper encoded messages said to Obama, "You're in denial—consciously 'ignorant.' But something very sinister went on in your life and you're behaving in a sinister way, not protecting America, much less the world,

11

from radical Islam terrorists. You can't even say the words—so something's wrong. Deep down you know why better than anyone. Tell us."

That's when Obama broke. Again he told us the real story in code. Secretly he longed to tell that story.

In a lengthy speech on June 14, an angry Obama unconsciously revealed precisely that he has a powerful mental block he does not understand. This explains his Middle East strategy and why he simply can't protect America.

Donald Trump struck a nerve. Obama, Trump later noted, was furious. Why? In reality, he was furious about being pressured to explain himself. Trump had tapped into something dark and deep in Obama, something he desperately hides. Yet also unconsciously Obama wants to reveal that dark secret.

Intuitively Trump knows that we all perceive far more than we realize consciously. As we've only recently learned clinically, Trump was alluding to the fact that we all have an unbelievably perceptive unconscious super intelligence. Obama will confess that he reads himself much better than he consciously knows and will unconsciously tell us that story. We all know it deep down. Trump knows it. Obama will confess that unconsciously Trump knows full well who he really is.

Obama refuses to get tough on terrorism

Obama begins his story with a major projection: he refuses to get tough on terrorism. He is all talk.

He tells us to make it harder for terrorists to use weapons to kill us. This is the same Obama who is the great arms enabler who aids enemies such as ISIS and the nation of Iran. His great unconscious super-intel will tell us why.

Consciously Obama focuses on banning guns in America, but in so doing his super-intel confesses unknowingly that he himself is the violent enabling force that threatens our country.

12

He mentions those on the other side of the aisle who criticize him for avoiding the term "radical Islam," alluding to his other side—his super-intel's moral compass.

He sees unconsciously his fundamental weakness. His refusal to use "radical Islam"—confirmed by strong actions—means he simply can't beat ISIS.

In a distinct projection he says exactly that, "…using the phrase 'radical Islam'…that's the key, they tell us [he tells himself]. We can't beat ISIL unless we call them radical Islamists." And he won't do it. Something about radical Islam contains the Rosetta Stone needed to fully understand Obama and what deep inside him controls his self-sabotaging decisions.

Indeed, that's "the key" to understanding him, what's behind his refusal to call the enemy who they are. Obama hints he's afraid to speak up to the enemy. He starts with his grand conclusion—"the key"—as he unconsciously underscores, "Let me make my final point."

A name reflects an identity—who someone is and who they aren't and how each is different. The fact that he won't call America's current most formidable enemy by its true name reflects his own lack of identity. The fact that he can't say who *they* are means he also can't say who *he* is. His identity is controlled by them.

His identity then becomes "puppet of radical Islam," a puppet who cannot name those who pull the strings, someone who cannot truly admit they are dangerous.

His non-personhood is confirmed by his true secret non-identity. Indirectly he calls himself by a secret name which he cannot say—radical Islamic sympathizer. This is a major clue that Obama is an unconscious Stockholm Syndrome victim. The term originated when captives in a bank robbery standoff in Sweden after a few days embraced completely the demands of their persecutors. Unconsciously brainwashed they "switched sides" to survive.

The one thing such a victim cannot do is confess, cannot speak up to their captors just as Obama can't speak up now.

Obama can't say the term because *he has been programmed unconsciously* not to say it, to continually submit to ISIS and radical Islam. As the story unfolds we will see the ultimate terror that shaped his life when he was a child—the hallmark of a Stockholm Syndrome.

To become a Stockholm Syndrome victim of radical Islam requires two terrifying events—entrapment and imminent death at the hands of a radical abusive Islamist. A certainty you will not survive. As Obama explains shortly, he had both.

Listen and you hear, deny it and you will never appreciate the danger Obama presents to America and the world. In fact, he's far more dangerous than a secret Muslim who hates America and knows it. He has completely rationalized his actions. He's in deep denial but his deeper mind shouts out his victimization.

Obama quickly presents a compelling picture of his secret Stockholm Syndrome identity. In projection code Obama declares, "if someone seriously thinks." In other words, his serious super-intel that thinks brilliantly, far ahead of his conscious blind spots, describes in rich denial imagery his classic Stockholm Syndrome: "I don't know who we're fighting…confused about who our enemies are." In a projection others imply he's not "taking the fight seriously" against ISIS.

Obama continues with numerous tells that he's unconsciously a full-fledged Stockholm Syndrome victim. He will tell us how he was radicalized—and how he buried it; the devastating effect he's had on America; and what America should do now. He will elaborate in a shocking conclusion. But first we must clearly understand the Stockholm Syndrome.

Patty Hearst story

The poster child for the Stockholm Syndrome remains Patty Hearst.

Everyone over a certain age recalls the 1974 photo on magazine covers around the world. If ever a picture said a thousand words this was it.

Newspaper heiress Patricia Hearst—a 19-year-old kidnapped college sophomore from Berkeley who had disappeared for months—suddenly is caught on a security camera robbing a bank with her terrorist captors the radical "left-wing" Symbionese Liberation Army. Here she is, a beret on her head, seriously pointing a rifle barking commands at bank customers having joined her former enemies in the heist. She had totally crossed over. Two people were shot in the robbery.

Over the next several months she made several public announcements released on tape proudly proclaiming she was now an SLA member joining their just cause. After 13 days in captivity, she was making demands for money and food distribution to the inner city. She ultimately denounced her former life, her parents and fiancé.

Eventually 19 months after her kidnapping, police captured her and her former abductors. She was later tried for her crimes while her attorneys claimed she had been brainwashed.

Her captors had immediately isolated her and constantly threatened to kill her, all the while vehemently proclaiming the justice of their movement. Petrified day after day of abuse, completely surrounded by her vicious enemy she finally broke. She totally merged her beliefs with her kidnappers, bought into to their commands and idealized them. She could now see plainly their just cause and meant it. Her mind-set was fixed—proving herself worthy by joining their terrorist crimes. Now she was safe. They trusted her. She had found the only way to save her life—but it was a costly decision.

It had taken her time after her arrest to begin seeing things clearly again. Slowly she became deprogrammed. But the jury was convinced by the horror of her crimes—she'd become an armed bank robber and member of a subversive group. She received a long prison sentence which was later commuted by President Jimmy Carter. She was finally pardoned years later by President Bill Clinton.

Yet she had truly become a Stockholm Syndrome believer who had gone to the mat for the SLA in the process risking her life at the hands of law enforcement.

Obama's Stockholm Syndrome worse than Hearst's

But Obama's Stockholm Syndrome is far more powerful and fixated than Patricia Hearst's. She could eventually recall the petrifying kidnapping and the rapid brainwashing. Obama had no conscious recall. His brainwashing happened so much earlier he totally buried the traumas. But it left him with his mind frozen in the perpetual "now" surrounded by his terrorists. A totally unconscious post-traumatic stress disorder of the worst kind.

He's still in that never-ending moment. He's Patty Hearst right after she capitulated. (Of course Obama can cover up his victimization and make minor concessions appearing presidential.) That's why he was so vulnerable to Trump's confrontation.

Obama confessing to Trump for years—and why

But he's also been looking to Trump unconsciously for several years—the one man who could finally help set Obama free. It's one of the strangest twists in any story in history. The super intelligence is a master story-teller that weaves together a cohesive narrative uncovering a deep drama no one can imagine. Obama's super-intel doesn't disappoint.

We return to Obama's secret story in this key speech.

Obama is continually speaking to Trump unconsciously in

code. Between the lines early in his June 14, 2016 speech he praised Trump for catching on, thus eliciting Obama's major confession.

He first stops to praise Trump, indirectly revealing powerful reasons he desperately needs Trump to get the story out—and rescue America. The stakes are that high.

Obama alludes to meeting with his new national security director "who will "intensify the campaign to destroy the terrorist group ISIL." But the phrase implies a question, "who will do this?"—and the answer: "I can't." It's a subliminal message that Trump was helping secure America by pressuring him. The only way Obama can help is by confessing unconsciously.

So in projection code Obama confesses he's unknowingly in silent partnership with ISIS, but that's changed if we can hear his instructions. His super-intel wants to intensify the campaign and destroy Obama's entrapment in his Stockholm Syndrome role.

His rich imagery elaborates on Trump's key role and pressure. "This campaign at this stage is firing on all cylinders...ISIL is under more pressure than ever before... ISIL continues to lose key leaders. They're on the run." Trump has Obama, the Stockholm Syndrome victim, on the run joining forces with Obama's vast super intelligence.

Obama's on an intense hidden confession campaign on two fronts. First he will identify his key Stockholm Syndrome role in not stopping ISIS and radical Islam. Far beyond that, he will confess that really he's the dangerous Stockholm Syndrome-controlled terrorist threatening America who must be stopped in a larger way. Hear his confession and it will change the world. Make it far safer if we can see, he's a Stockholm Syndrome victim who deep down despises the role.

Obama's super-intel has just ratcheted up the fight, and the plan's humming along. Obama's preparing to sing big time.

Pay extremely close attention to his words, "this campaign at this stage is firing" suggests that Obama is about to figuratively fire himself again, stressing that a campaign of some sort will be necessary. He will return later to the punch line in his speech, to precisely define "firing." It will be a battle won in stages—if it's won at all.

Nobody gets to Obama as Trump does. Donald Trump is the one man to whom he wants to confess, the one man who can stop him if Trump takes on the right leadership role. In effect Obama calls Trump America's symbolic national security director.

He later implies Trump should be president—specifically noting he was the Republican nominee. *In fact Trump is the secret Obama nominee who can carry out the ultimate plan Obama will lay out.* Trump's the one leader in America who has demonstrated the skill and grasps the need.

Moments like this in Obama's secret story highlight just how far Obama's unconscious mind, a completely separate intelligence, is from his conscious mind which constantly ridicules Trump. Who can believe this shocking drama with twists like America could never imagine in her worst dream? Believe it—Obama does.

He also knows Hillary Clinton as president would continue his Stockholm Syndrome enslavement to radical Islam. Only Trump knows the path for Obama's freedom and America's.

This explains why Obama's media is so terrified and must attack Trump. They have embraced a myth out of their own needs. Imagine: they have overlooked a Stockholm Syndrome victim of radical Islam in office, fulling embracing his propaganda campaign of Islamophobia.

Stockholm Syndrome repercussions

He then demonstrates his distorted decision-making. In denial—calling it a "surprise"—he speaks of the "thousands of

18

terrorists who we've taken off the battlefield." But in reality he put thousands of terrorists on the battlefield enabling ISIS by taking thousands of U.S. troops off the battlefield in Iraq against strong objections by military advisors. As a Stockholm Syndrome victim he was unconsciously programmed to see American troops as the enemy—exactly matching his behavior and his decisions.

Next he speaks of thousands of soldiers working to defeat ISIS and spending seven years "dismantling al-Qaeda." The truth is, as John McCain noted, that Obama rebuilt al-Qaeda as ISIS. He's the new founder of ISIS. Trump was right when he said that, too.

Notice Obama's refuses to say the acronym "ISIS" (Islamic State in Iraq and Syria) instead using "ISIL" ("Islamic State of Iraq and the Levant") which means dominant over the entire eastern shore of the Mediterranean Sea. He gives the radical Islam terrorist group far more power than they have again reflecting his Stockholm Syndrome instructions.

In another denial confession of his startlingly passive strategy, Obama alludes to his inadequate special forces' ongoing efforts at defeating ISIS on the ground. What he's admitting is that he has no real ground troops. He removed them all. Blindly Obama rationalizes his actions.

The enabling Stockholm Syndrome president

Yet in vivid projection code Obama explains his main cover—the central disguised method of subversive actions by which he carries out his Stockholm Syndrome mission. He describes, "addressing larger forces *that have allowed these terrorists* to gain traction in parts of the world." In other words, as the most powerful man in the world, he admits it was he himself who is the larger force continually enabling terrorists "to gain traction" around the world.

Quickly Obama provides the major insight to decode his

decisions, "unconscious enabling"—the foundation of his disguised saboteur role.

As a Stockholm Syndrome president he is ISIS deep down. He enables their secret violence. He may take minimal "JV" actions against them because he must see them as the "JV."

Consider everything about terrorists in this speech a projection, what Obama has enabled—a part of him. And you will understand he's a secret Stockholm Syndrome even from himself.

Stockholm Syndrome strategy: four key Obama denials

We return to his projected confession that he can't beat ISIS unless he calls them radical Islamists. In four key denials he explains why.

Obama asks four rhetorical questions which all deny that using "radical Islam" is important—all of which plainly identify him as a Stockholm Syndrome victim. He describes what would happen if he could see past the powerful blind spot.

We read through the denials to see the truth.

First, "What exactly would using this label accomplish, exactly what would it change?" He's really saying that it would change everything…if he meant it—if he could only do it. His subsequent denial questions tell us exactly what would change—and why he can't.

Secondly, he asks, "Would it make ISIL less committed to trying to kill Americans?" In code he answers, "of course it would." Unknowingly Obama confesses that he has empowered ISIS, allowing them to kill Americans. It's easy to see—Barack Hussein Obama is the very embodiment of a Stockholm Syndrome victim secretly committed to the enemy.

Thirdly, "Would it bring in more allies?" His super-intel answers. It would bring in America—the great power he continually blocks with his half-hearted efforts. To see who he was would take away the most powerful ally that ISIS has—Obama, Stockholm Syndrome victim and their founder.

Finally, he answers the crucial question everyone wants to know: "Is there a military strategy that is served by this?" Obama confesses his secret "do-nothing" military strategy "does everything" for radical Islam, constantly enabling it. He has been a radical Islam president from start to finish. His strategy has severely hurt America and the world.

Obama confesses that if he actually owned up to who he is and how he has been unconsciously controlled by them—it would make him less violent, an American ally finally, and it would drastically change his strategy. He'd put boots on the ground that really stop ISIS. He never would have empowered them in first place. Deep down he would like to change. Here we see the result of early brainwashing.

Unconsciously Obama emphasizes his Stockholm Syndrome enslavement with two more denials—six in all. "The answer is none of the above. Calling a threat by a different name does not make it go away. This is a political distraction." In other words, the answer as to why he can't say "radical Islam" is all of the above ways by which he's totally controlled by ISIS.

Which Obama decisions regarding radical Islam do not fit a Stockholm Syndrome president? Recently he even paid terrorist Iran $400 million dollars in cash as a ransom for four American prisoners—and then denied that it was a ransom.

The danger—a new story

Many will say they knew all along Obama was a secret Muslim who hated America. His super intelligence, however, takes us far deeper.

He has Muslim sympathies and resents the U.S., but he's totally unaware of how his mind's controlled by his abuser.

Obama does not see who he is consciously—making him far more dangerous as a leader. He's completely programmed, meaning he has no idea where to stop. Think about it. Think about the nuclear deal with Iran—Obama, the Stockholm Syndrome victim, believing he's saving the world. He has completely rationalized his actions making his ability to convince others of his deceitful plans far more believable.

Even to this point we see how Donald Trump's perceptive intuition has elicited a powerful confession. Nowhere else in all his communications does Obama reveal so clearly his true strategy in the Middle East and his extreme Stockholm Syndrome victimization.

Trump is picking up far more than he consciously knows. Thanks to our own brilliant super intelligence, everyone knows the story Obama's telling. We've lived it for eight years. Later we will see that several prominent journalists also unconsciously know.

The reality that Obama's truly a Stockholm Syndrome president simply reveals the ability people have to live in denial with uncomfortable truths. Why in a very real way we need divine help every bit as much as our founders did. As Scripture declares, "Get wisdom: and with all thy getting get understanding." (Proverbs 4:7) The newly discovered super-intel helps us all see past blind spots.

Obama himself is a masterful distractor, using politics and personal ideology to distract. He appears to be a politician, but he's a secret pawn. He presents a super-intel confession of being totally unconsciously distracted from being a president truly attentive to America. Instead, he's distracted by an unspeakable inner terror, distracted from being a true individual and distracted by his radical Islam abuser(s) who insist he live out his assigned role.

How Obama was radicalized

When Obama enables radical Islam, he points to how—as a youth—he was radicalized and controlled by a violent Muslim—whose identity will become clear.

22

He tells us how ISIS radicalizes its victims, suggesting exactly what happened to him. Their primary tactic is fear and abuse as Obama describes how he was brainwashed.

First in a projection he speaks of abuse in America's history alluding to his own severely abusive background. Then he elaborates specifically on how radical Islam controls its victims.

The key is to understand he's unconsciously constantly fixated with the terrorists who violently brainwashed him as a child. Understand that *fear* is the single-most important issue at the core of the Stockholm Syndrome.

He describes his history of being terrorized, "We've [I've] gone through moments in our [my] history before when we [I] acted out of fear, and we came to regret it." He's talking about himself. Obama admits he constantly acts out of fear due to a severe event in his past. He could only refer to one time in his life when he was exposed to radical Islam, when he could have been victimized to this degree.

He explains, "We've [He's] seen our government [his governor] mistreat…fellow citizens [him], and it has been a shameful part of our [my] history." He's saying the authority figure(s) who governed Obama's young life deeply abused him, leaving him engulfed in shame. Somebody shamed his very existence. The repeat message marker "(my) history" underscores the crucial matter—*instructing us to examine Obama's personal history closely.* Such total domination over him suggests it occurred early in his life when he was most vulnerable to being mistreated by an Islamic authority figure.

Perfect picture of a soft, young target

Looking back at a November 2015 speech, Obama presented a key denial confession of the history of his Stockholm Syndrome terror and it matches this current speech. He reassured Americans they had nothing to fear from ISIS. Between the lines he revealed specifically how his early childhood brainwashing occurred leading to his Stockholm Syndrome with its accompanying massive denial,

"Groups like ISIL cannot defeat us on the battlefield, *so they try to terrorize us at home—against soft targets, against civilians, against innocent people.* Even as we're vigilant, we cannot, and we will not, subcumb [sic] to fear. Nor can we allow fear to divide us—for that's how terrorists win. We cannot give them the victory of changing how we go about living our lives."

Obama lays it all out: he was an innocent, soft target *terrorized at home.* His Islamic terrorist won with a total victory changing how a defeated Obama lived out his life from then on. His multiple denials confirm that he completely "subcumb(ed)" [sic] to fear—his slip pointing to the buried subconscious horror and yielding to the vastly superior force. It left him a completely divided "sub-person"—never truly an individual constantly enslaved to radical Islam, the perfect Stockholm Syndrome. Eventually he would become a sub-president for America—constantly performing sub-par but an excellent Stockholm Syndrome president.

Was he also confessing he was a "substitute" president—an illegal one? Would he carry his Stockholm Syndrome role that far aided by Saul Alinsky, his later surrogate terrorist programmer? He will soon answer this question. Above all Obama points to being brainwashed at a very young age.

Obama denies his terror

But Obama denies the massive terror that controls him. After every terrorist attack here and around the world he repeatedly tells Americans, "don't fear ISIS," misleading his own constituents—urging all of us to adopt his denial.

He reveals his illogical thinking—his desperate blind spot. We acted out of fear in WW II and took action that saved the free world. But unconsciously he "regrets"—despises—the fear that controls him revealing the unconscious stranglehold it has on him. How much he's a Stockholm Syndrome president and how blind he is to it—brainwashed by his terrorist.

His comment, "don't fear ISIS," also declares, "don't fear me—the great enabler of ISIS." Read through the denial further, he warns us, "Fear me." Indeed, we must. As the most powerful man in the world, an embedded pawn of radical Islam, he is very simply the most dangerous man in the world. Just as his abuser was the most dangerous and powerful man in the world to him.

Father the abuser

What 'radical Islamist" could have terrorized Obama so, abused him beyond belief? Looking closely at Obama's biography, it's clear that only one primary person in his life exists connected to Islam who programmed him in his home environment.

His Muslim father wanted him aborted, didn't want his half-white son at all, abandoning him at birth. (This was extensively documented in my previous book, *The Obama Confession, Secret Fear, Secret Fury."*)[2] Obama's father was discouraged by his own abusive Muslim father who objected to his plans to marry Obama's white American mother. In fact, his own father despised Obama's white blood and by implication Obama would later conclude his non-Muslim blood from his mother's side.

This near-abortion was the deepest shame imaginable and became deeper still when Obama figured out unconsciously that his mother was in on it. She came close to carrying out the abortion.

Kids always unconsciously learn the family secrets. Obama reveals deep down he saw the whole story—more recently confirmed by his severe behavior.

---

[2] Andrew G. Hodges, *The Obama Confession: Secret Fear, Secret Fury*, Village House Publishers, 2012.

As Obama put the story together with one horrific revelation after another, each one worse than the last, it became one constant recreation of the events. Leaving him more and more convinced he was about to be killed "again."

Obama saw his father only once in his life, at age 10 for two weeks. His father was a violent man who abused Obama's mother along with two other wives. It's also likely he never legally married Obama's mother.

To want your son aborted and to completely abandon him at birth are murderous acts as Obama experienced them. Although he would realize them unconsciously, he had to deny them. But frozen in his mind, his father was the radical Islamist terrorist who wanted to destroy him. Stockholm Syndrome victim experiences represent a subconscious frozen post-traumatic stress disorder. The victim believes he will be killed unless he totally submits. The terrorist says, "Stand up to me in any way, including calling me a terrorist, and I will kill you. Go along with my wishes, become like me, and you live." So Obama unconsciously identified with the aggressor and submitted at every turn.

Fathers' Day 2008—Obama recalls his destruction

Obama has been trying to take us back to his early life for years, to share the sad story about the origin of his Stockholm Syndrome victimization. Therapists know well that adults and children both relate key stories that tell who they are.

Go back to his Father's Day speech as a presidential candidate delivered on Easter Sunday in April 2008. He described how fathers use their uniquely powerful role to build kids. He used Jesus' biblical parable to contrast the kid whose home—whose life—was built on something solid (rock) with the kid whose life was built on a weak foundation (nothing but sand). The peak drama was the matter of which one of the two could make it through the severe storms of life. Even deeper he implied only one would live. Only the one who was built

26

on the laws/foundations of the solid home and a nurturing father could stand up to those difficulties.

Obama specifically mentioned his own father who left him early in life causing him great difficulty. Indirectly he told the world, "My father assaulted my very being, my very foundation as if I were blown to kingdom come and never even existed. Like sand blowing in the wind." *He painted a vivid picture of his abortion the father wanted carried out.* His father completed the message when he totally abandoned him from birth. Subconsciously Obama could still see his father's abuse now in real time—frozen in his mind. On the verge of happening again and again.

Deep down he had spelled out the life-threatening event that took place in his home very early when he was a soft target.

His father was unquestionably a violent man with a long history of spousal abuse, child abuse and abusing others. He would die in his third drunk-driving car wreck crashing into a tree after he had first killed a man and later lost his own legs in two previous such accidents.

A president leads a nation through severe storms—the captain of the ship must take charge of the sails and the rudder. Obama unconsciously was telling us that he would not lead America in secure directions. He had been groomed instead to enact his abuser's program to shipwreck America.

He would attack America's very foundations. Smoothly he would call his disruptions "hope and change," rationalizing the secret Stockholm Syndrome storm that raged inside him. But keep the keyword "foundation" in mind—and think about America's true foundations. Obama surely did during his two terms as president.

Abusive father becomes Islam to Obama

Now for the other part of Obama's great secret. He tells you how he was radicalized by Islam and ISIS. *Whenever he looks at his father he sees Islam personified.* He cannot distinguish between Muslims and radical Islamic terrorists. To him, they are one and the same. He's totally controlled by them just as he was thoroughly controlled by his father.

At such an early age his abusive father was the whole world to the son. With his violent personality and Muslim ethnicity, the two fused into one for Obama.

In his mind, Islam or radical Islam became Obama's surrogate father. He always saw his father as a radical Muslim and deep down he cannot differentiate peace-loving Muslims from violent Muslims. That's why to this day he constantly submits to both.

His later childhood experience living in Indonesia for several years with his mother and Muslim step-father, Lolo Soetero, would verify in his mind that Islam could be dangerous thus confirming his programming. Now he could see it for real.

His step-father told him all about his war experiences as a solder. Whereupon Obama specifically asked him if he had ever killed a man—indicating the "father who kills" is buried deep in his mind. His step-father said he had indeed killed other men—another discomforting reality for the impressionable young Obama. And when his mother divorced his step-father, that reminded Obama again of father abandonment. Obama had taken his step-father's name and was called Barry Soetero for years magnifying the loss.

He never recovered from the abusive father on so many levels. He was the perfect candidate to become a Stockholm Syndrome radical Islamist prisoner.

The earlier the terror the greater it can become. And for radical Islam all the better. Obama buried his father terror deeper than we can imagine in his unconscious.

His mother was in on it to some degree. She wanted to abort him after she carelessly got pregnant by his Muslim father, the man she'd selected. It was a devastating team. Despite her efforts to idealize his father, young Obama found the facts far too consuming. She also abandoned Obama herself later to return to the East.

These significant traumas shaped his destiny.

Stockholm Syndrome president 'doing the terrorists' work for them'

Obama unconsciously tells us specifically how he was "recruited" by his terrorist father's Muslim authority.

The vulnerable Obama was convinced "he" speak(s) for Islam, a billion-plus people, "their propaganda…how they recruit."

In Obama's mind his father the terrorist claimed he was "the true leader(s) of …a billion Muslims…who reject…[his] crazy notions," but Obama couldn't. In his young mind his father was The Leader of all Muslims—it was all Obama knew about them. In another phrase Obama pictures his brainwashed mind, someone who "suggests entire religious communities are complicit in violence." Again, his father represented radical Islam itself.

He fell "into the trap of painting all Muslims with a broad brush." Subconsciously radicalized by his father—all Islam to Obama.

His extremely abusive father in essence singled Obama out to carry out Stockholm Syndrome Islamic violence. Obama describes perfectly his enabling role—"complicit in violence."

Obama was convinced he was "at war with an entire religion," and now totally under his father's control.

Then he was fixated on "doing the terrorists' work for them." That's the clearest single description of his secret Stockholm Syndrome role. And he was carrying it out per instructions: keep them unidentified. Never say their name. That's why he avoids saying "radical Islam" to this day.

In (denial) code Obama adds another picture of his powerful programmed role as a secret terrorist (of "groups like

29

ISIS"). He was instructed secretly "to make this war a war between Islam and America, Islam and the West" with Islam the aggressor.

Eyes always on father and abuse

In his memoir, *Dreams from My Father,* Obama described the only visit he ever had with his father when the youngster was a 10-year-old elementary school student in Hawaii. Obama's father spoke to his son's class about the warrior tribe he was from in Kenya. Deep down Obama saw his father as a terrifying warrior who could track him down all the way to America.

By this age Obama had already put the story together in the back of his mind that his father had wanted him to destroy him. He would have heard his father's story as a secret confession that his father the warrior actually tried to kill him in person at his birth. His father hints this occurred in Kenya.

The super-intel has taught us far more than we ever previously knew about severe PTSD. A trauma victim never takes his eyes off what happened to him. In Obama's case his unconscious eyes remain constantly on his father's abuse—frozen in that mode in a living day-by-day distraction. This is the trigger to explain Obama's repetitive thought patterns now and in multiple other communications. Many times he describes unknowingly how he behaves like his father who's never out of his sight. Only his super-intel—using vivid imagery—can reveal his deepest buried trauma.

Obama, the terrified youth in the West

Even when he got away from his father, Obama's mind-set was already fixed, dominated by that vision. Even when he was in the West and his father thousands of miles away, they were never really separated. Obama escaped from his father who returned to Kenya, but while living with his mother in America, deep down he still saw himself in great danger.

When it's frozen in your mind that your father wants to kill you, and it almost happened—and you feel like he had killed you by walking away—it was so real it *did* happen. Alive but barely, the child naturally suspects the father will return to finish him off. Frozen PTSD—that was Obama's mind. He alludes to it in his speech as a "Muslim in America" being "constantly under suspicion and under attack."

Over time Obama learned the truth about his father, mother and their dysfunctional relationship. His father, the communist who hates the West, was now living in his native Kenya. Young Barack learned of all the chaos surrounding his birth. His 18-year-old countercultural mother suddenly leaving his abusive father in Hawaii immediately after his birth, escaping to Seattle. She only returned to her Hawaiian home a year later, after Obama Sr. graduated.

Obama had a clear picture his of his father as a Kenyan. He began to suspect unconsciously that powerful, near-murderous events directed at his mother and him around his birth occurred in Kenya not Hawaii—where his father showed his true colors. This prompted his mother to urgently get them both as far away from Obama Sr. as possible. Later he tells us he had picked up on family stories that he had been born in Kenya.

Obama Sr. was a Muslim who was vehemently anti-Western. Obama Jr. was left alone and vulnerable in America. Now living in the West with his mother, Obama feared his father's far-reaching rage for another reason. Simply living in the West, the U.S., was enough to further enrage his father who saw all Westerners as Muslim-haters.

Obama mentions his fear, "fueling ISIL's notion that the West hates Muslims."

He links this idea specifically as to why he can never utter the words, "radical Islam"—making the frozen monster father in his mind even more dangerous. He could never call his father a name. Now as a Stockholm Syndrome president he

31

deeply fears ISIS—his surrogate Islamist father—and fuels their rage enabling them to explode through the Middle East.

Even as a total radical Islam sympathizer and Stockholm Syndrome victim, Obama is never safe in his mind. Constantly reminded, re-experiencing unconscious flashbacks that his father, or substitute father figure radical Islam, was about to attack him.

In more projection code, he describes himself as a youth struggling with his Muslim identity in America, "young Muslims in this country and around the world feel like, no matter what they do, they're going to be under suspicion and under attack."

The term "radical Islam" evokes a "life or death" phobia in Obama. He must be extra careful, always on guard with any words referencing Islam.

Islam itself and Obama

The Muslim religion would have played directly into Obama's Stockholm Syndrome. He would see his father was speaking for Allah when he said either you embrace Islam fully or die as an infidel. No wonder Obama's Muslim sympathies are so blatant. No wonder he made a slip of the tongue alluding to "my Muslim faith" when speaking about his Christian faith as a presidential candidate in front of millions no less. On other occasions he embraces both, stating there are different ways of getting to God. At best Obama's confused about his religion, but deep down he must remain steadfast to Islam. He has to insist the Muslim call to prayer "is the most beautiful sound in the world." You see, his father never uttered anything but beautiful words to him in Obama's conscious mind. He must do the same.

In his fear state, Obama makes plain that he could not under any circumstances overtly express anger at his father or mother over what they had done to him. He was constantly "under suspicion and under attack." That's exactly what we now see in Obama who repeatedly fails to stand up to radical Islam.

How well this fits with Thomas Sowell's view of Obama. The perceptive columnist predicts that—if Iran bombed America with a nuclear weapon—Obama would totally capitulate and surrender. It would be his Stockholm Syndrome in maximum action.

But imagine the anger he could never express toward his emotional captor(s). Obama was furious with his father which scared him even more. What does he do with that fury? Like a good Stockholm Syndrome soldier he simply displaces his rage onto the West and our own United States.

Obama's buried rage against father

He mentions "the special forces that I ordered to get bin Laden." This points to his buried rage at his father expressed by killing the symbolic Islamist father-figure terrorist just as Obama's father killed him. Only by displacing his fury could Obama express his anger which he normally takes out on the U.S. and "The West" (our western allies) as a secret Stockholm Syndrome troop. Obama utilizes Bin Laden's killing as a magic cover for his extensive foreign-policy deceit.

At the same time Obama constantly projects his rage at his Islamic terrorist father onto America accusing us all of being anti-Muslim.

Saul Alinsky recalled

Obama's Stockholm Syndrome explains why, as a young man, he experienced a powerful magnetic pull to the radical anarchist Saul Alinsky as a surrogate father.

Alinsky advocated the overthrow of America—secretly from the inside. Obama alludes to this in his June 14 speech by mentioning an angry young man in college.

Unconsciously fixated in the role of being controlled,

Obama was looking for a new controller who could help him carry out his sabotage of America and the West. He was a perfect fit for Alinsky's model of deceit: secretly sabotaging from within while appearing to embrace societal norms and stability. This was exactly how Obama's father and primary programmer treated him. Obama was told as a young child his father embraced him and his mother—despite the divorce. In the end Obama unconsciously learned his father was an anarchist who destroyed everything and everybody he touched: his home life abusing his various wives and kids, his academic program, his career, other people and eventually himself.

Obama the Stockholm Syndrome president will eventually reflect that anarchy in his Iran nuclear deal arming radical Islamists extremists who well might blow up the world and themselves "accidentally" in their rage. Big-time suicidal bombers. Previously Obama had become an Alinsky trainer, and now as a Stockholm Syndrome president he trained enough American and world leaders to follow his destructive plans.

'Do-nothing' Stockholm Syndrome strategy linked to father

He reveals just how entrenched his submissive Stockholm Syndrome victim role is with five more denials indirectly linked to his "advisor father." He confesses never a "moment in my seven and a half years as president where [I] have…been able to pursue a strategy" against radical Islam. Maximum denial. That's the Stockholm Syndrome at its absolute—since the day he took office.

We can hear his father's commands as his number-one inner adviser that he dare not attack Islamic terrorists, never even utter the term, "Not once has an adviser of mine said, 'Man… really use that phrase, we're going to turn this whole thing around. Not once." Read his denial confession: not

34

once—saying it twice—did his chief advisor (father) allow him to use that phrase. Following orders, not once has Obama really turned things around on radical Islam despite his political rhetoric.

Instead he's the Stockholm Syndrome president who has turned the whole thing around on America, constantly defending Islam. His father was the game-changer in his life that Obama has never turned down—the one who absolutely forbade Obama under the sentence of death from ever using the term. But reading through his denials, Obama subconsciously knows in a heartbeat he could (and should) completely defeat ISIS and radical Islam if he so chose—and be his own man, a real man, for the first time.

Yet as a good Stockholm Syndrome president he started his presidency with an immediate apology tour to Islamic countries secretly announcing in effect, "Don't worry, I'm one of you. You're entirely a great religion of peace and Muhammad was a holy prophet and I will never deviate from that stance. I will assure the world I can win you over and Islam will love me. When radical Islamic terrorists show up I will make sure they have no connection to Islam, denounce anyone who says so—obfuscate at every attack." Obama must incessantly deny Islam's connection to terrorists, declaring it's a religion of peace to continually bury his utter terror of his Muslim father.

Obama wanted no accountability for his actions, simply explaining it away as his brand of "new politics," the greatest political distraction in American history. Who could believe it was possible? A radical Islam mole now lived in the White House, a man who didn't consciously know it himself. That's the power of the wounded unconscious controlled by the worst PTSD imaginable.

Obama, the secret Islamic terrorist sympathizer, was now programmed to believe he could do what he wanted without accountability—using the cover of "smart politics" at will.

Only by submitting to his unconscious wisdom and facing his terror could Obama change. Yet he knows nothing about his super-intel and is not about to learn. He's certain his conscious mind knows everything and he fears accountability for his actions.

Father terror persists

Obama continues linking his inability to use the words "radical Islam" to his Stockholm Syndrome and to his terrifying father.

You call a horrific threat by a different name when you take strong, meaningful actions against them. Only then do they go away. Obama's obstinate refusal to speak the words "radical Islam" reflects how terrified he is of them. That explains his enormous passivity in the face of worldwide terrorist threats. His passive words reflect his passive actions—his deep Stockholm Syndrome. Meanwhile, his cover-up words of denial are the real political distraction— distracting America and himself from the reality of being a prisoner to radical Islam. He can't say "radical Islam" because it's too close to his prison name, Stockholm Syndrome victim something he was forbidden to admit. He can only say presidential political distraction.

Return to his statement, "Calling a threat by a different name does not make it go away." He cannot rid himself of his ever-present consuming father haunting his deep psyche.

In vivid imagery Obama elaborates on his core strategy. Deep down he tells us, "...[I] know the nature of the enemy" alluding to his father, radical Islam personified.

He's careful because it "has everything to do with actually defeating extremism," defeating America, the extremist enemy in his Muslim father's eyes—exactly the plan Obama unconsciously carries out.

Think again of kidnap victim Patricia Hearst—a Stockholm Syndrome victim robbing a bank. To survive that situation, she had to be convincing. She had to aim that weapon as if she meant to use it—and so does Obama. That's how deep he's in. Deviate and you die.

Obama had to be politically correct about "radical Islam" to survive—the true reason he won't say it. Wherever it's found, political correctness means no boundaries, no judgement, no identity. No wonder Obama has been the PC president personified.

Again in denial code Obama continues spelling out details of his massive Stockholm Syndrome attack on the nation. He has "prevented folks across the government from doing their jobs, from sacrificing and working really hard to protect the American people."

Obama Stockholm Syndrome attacks

Barack Obama has prevented police and military from calling Islamist terrorist suspects by name. His administration has deleted references to Islam's violent nature from FBI counter-terrorism training manuals.

In projection code Obama confesses "how dangerous... [his Stockholm Syndrome] mind-set and thinking can be"—as he secretly embraces Islam. His "loose talk and sloppiness about who exactly we're fighting, where it can lead." Who— exactly—are we fighting, indeed? He admits unconsciously that his Stockholm Syndrome thinking leaves him unbelievably sloppy about the enemy's actual identity.

He alludes to people starting to see that he continues leading America into more and more danger. *But don't overlook the key message: his mind is fixated in constant danger: another Stockholm Syndrome image.*

Media misses Obama's messages

In his June speeches following the nightclub massacre in Orlando Obama tried to tell the media and America that his background was hugely important: do a background check.

The media's reaction: We don't do deeper motivation and background checks; we can't understand the message so move on. They are untrained and unconsciously want to avoid it. They failed to pay attention to Gladwell's bestseller, *Blink,* which introduced a dazzling new unconscious that quick-reads situations clinically called unconscious perception. They are unaware of the newly discovered super intelligence that reveals valuable new information—and are disinclined to learn how it spells out the details of abuse revealing dysfunctional traits in a leader.

Who wants to see a presidential candidate this wounded, his life so troubled—especially the superhero Obama, the first black president? Many specifically criticized him for being too tough on African-American fathers in his 2008 Fathers' Day talk—when he was telling them all about his background as a victim of abuse.

We can also see why the media misses the full story of Obama's chief strategy: as an adult president enabling violence in others—especially radical Islam. Lacking super-intel awareness, they are not trained to understand unconscious communication and how Obama's super-intel has specifically confessed in projection code to enabling Islamic terrorists. At times the media will allude to his enabling but overlook how Obama's subconscious pleas insisting that it's far more extensive than they know. They have no idea that deep down he's constantly quick-reading himself and "quick-telling" what he sees.

The understanding among psychotherapists that horrific backgrounds such as Obama's hold powerful sway over a person's life is simply minimized by the media. The essential story Obama confesses, that he's truly a Stockholm Syndrome prisoner to his severe early abuse, is inaccessible to the media. They can't hear background stories—precisely where his great secret remains.

There's great hope, however, for the media. What their

conscious mind misses their own super-intel picks up. When Barack Obama's super-intel spoke between the lines of his June speeches, Donald Trump's super-intel picked up on the unconsciously delivered messages. Similarly, we will see later how many in the elite media intuited the truth about Obama's presidency. We all perceive far more than we realize consciously.

2

Obama Confesses To Illegal Presidency

More guidance in code: Terrorists among us

In another plethora of back-to-back denials, Obama unconsciously confesses what America should do to overcome his Stockholm Syndrome policies.

First, "where does this stop" declares "enough, America, stop me."

Obama confesses that radical Islam embedded terrorists who were "U.S. citizens" carried out mass murders (Fort Hood, San Bernardino, Orlando). But all put out warning signals which were poorly investigated as a direct result of Obama's secret pro-terrorist polices.

There's even more reason to stress that radical Islamists walk among us. Americans need to be more attuned to the threat. In Orlando, three years before he murdered dozens of nightclub patrons, terrorist Omar Mateen had told coworkers that his family had ties to al-Qaeda. The Obama's Justice Department investigated but closed the probe after a few months. The subsequent mass shooting could very likely have been prevented.

In a series of denial questions such as "Are we going to start treating all Muslim Americans differently?" his super-intel implies the obvious: start investigating differently all Muslim Americans who put out terrorist warnings. And he's especially pointing to himself as a secret Stockholm Syndrome victim: look at him differently.

Obama's distorted thinking is obvious in another denial asking, *"start discriminating against them, because of their faith?"* Unconsciously he advises the exact opposite: discriminate—assess—what kind of faith. Both radical Islamic terrorists and peaceful Muslims have a strong faith. It's dangerous not to differentiate between the two even seeking peaceful Muslims help in identifying the minority "radical Muslims." He implies that we look closely at whose faith he enables pointing to radical Islam.

His denial image, "Start treating all Muslim Americans differently" further implies "yes" in the sense of enlisting help from the entire Muslim community in identifying Muslims demonstrating signs they've been radicalized.

He makes the strongest case of calling out radical Islamists—to make America safer. Again he points toward himself as a radicalized Stockholm Syndrome victim.

Notice Obama's subtle confession in his repetitive command "start doing this." He's admitting how he "stopped doing this" in his undercover role handicapping investigations far and wide to enable radical Islam. This is also where we stop his Stockholm Syndrome behavior—recognize his absolutely dangerous sloppy thinking. Recognize also how he never started acting in America's best interest from the get-go.

But Obama's clear super-intel message is recognizing Islam presents a danger in America. Such awareness reflects "our Democratic ideals and makes us safe." The exact opposite of what the embedded Stockholm Syndrome victim, the radical Islam-controlled Obama enacts as he continues to threaten national security-- his secret mission from the get-go.

Obama, the Stockholm Syndrome president, also wants to bring in thousands of undifferentiated Muslims knowing full well that radical Islamists will be among them. Obama then attacks Trump, trying hard to manipulate Republican officials into confronting the presumptive GOP nominee. "Do Republican officials actually agree with this?" Reading through the denial, we see that Obama realizes deep down that Trump's proposal to stringently vet Muslim immigration should be instituted.

Indirectly he suggests Trump's truly presidential—the only man really onto him.

Obama confesses ultimate Stockholm Syndrome attack: illegal president

In a sequence of communications Obama now takes us to his ultimate Stockholm Syndrome attack on America. Not only has he continually enabled radical Islam in America, he has carried out the ultimate attack on America personally.

Look back over his recent denial and projection code images. First consider his reference that these embedded terrorists were U.S. citizens. *But all of these people— embedded terrorists—had a phony citizenship whose true loyalty was to radical Islam in the east.* Obama's imagery clearly points to him as a Stockholm Syndrome president whose true emotional citizenship is elsewhere but more. He strongly suggests he's not an American citizen and thus an illegal president.

He strongly validates this confession in numerous ways in a fascinating sequence.

Remember that immediately prior he asked, "where does this stop," suggesting that America should put an end— "stop"—his illegal presidency.

Look more closely at his denial instructions on the treatment of Muslim-Americans. First, "start treating them differently," translated he advises that we treat him very differently, as an illegal president. Next he advises us to "put them under special surveillance." Indirectly he calls for a special investigation of his ineligibility to become president. Obama's super-intel carefully builds this case with repeat unconscious messages using persuasive imagery.

He tells us "start discriminating *against them, because of their faith.*" In other words, discriminate—assess—whether his illegal presidency has enabled him to be favorable toward the Muslim faith. Hasn't he functioned as a proxy Muslim president? He has indeed. He seems to be confessing that in his heart he remains true to his original Muslim faith back in Indonesia. Surely his Stockholm Syndrome programming caused him to run as an illegal president. What better way to empower radical Islam than as the leader of the free world?

Unquestionably he could never have significantly enacted his Stockholm Syndrome agenda without the presidency. As a senator he could only vote against the initial war in Iraq—and now it comes into focus why, as a secret Stockholm Syndrome victim, he was the only one who opposed it.

His repeat command "start" means start a serious investigation of his illegal presidency. Plainly he's declaring the facts. No governing authority has seriously examined the only birth certificate he ever produced which was in 2011. Unofficial experienced document examiners declared it a phony. *Prior to that no one in the world had seen the alleged birth certificate.*

The fact that he produced it under duress speaks volumes as does the fact that it was forensic evidence that can be examined for signs of forgery—a sign of guilt. But also a sign that he really *wanted* to be discovered. That deep desire matches his repeated calls to stop him. Three years into his presidency Obama could have simply refused to produce a birth certificate—totally supported by his lap-dog media.

In this speech Obama's repeated subconscious calls for a complete investigation of his citizenship using powerful imagery are a distinct confession that he is an illegal president. He will continue this powerful message. In one sense the stakes are much higher now given his empowering of terrorists.

In the same vein Obama also makes reference to Trump using "language that singles out immigrants...entire religious communities...complicit in violence." Unknowingly he's a Stockholm Syndrome president, a lone immigrant, who has enabled radical Islam violence.

Obama ties stolen presidency to his father

In another brief vignette from his June 14, 2016 speech Obama provides a glimpse into how his abusive father still controls him in his deep psyche. After being prompted by Trump he finally comments about the true nature of ISIS warriors alluding to how he's been programmed. "Once again, ISIL's true nature has been revealed....These are not religious warriors, they are thugs and they are thieves." Earlier he mentioned how an inside ISIS source who was now confessing called their leaders thieves. He points to his super-intel inside source that sees the truth about his life.

He implies first his radical leader, his father, who programmed him stole his life brain-washing him into a Stockholm Syndrome robot. We can hear the image of his father, "religious warrior," who still controls his mind.

But Obama's also describing in a projection his secret role. In turn Obama follows the script and steals the presidency. He's the leader who steals. Here he ties his radical Islam programming and his illegal presidency together. He continues to confirm Trump's onto him.

His ultimate Stockholm Syndrome message: radical Islamists will win

Come back to Obama's denial confession—"We don't have religious tests here."

Of course we *do* have religious tests. We identify radical Islamists and put them on a watch list, and if they commit violence on behalf of their religion, we hold them accountable. But Obama has done all in his power to prevent such identification in law enforcement and in the military. He makes it easier for them to hide.

He reminds us of how he refused to label Fort Hood shooter Major Nidal Malik Hasan an Islamist terrorist even though Hasan had a well-documented association with Yemini-American terrorist recruiter Anwar al-Awlaki. He rationalizes that his "freedom of religion" empowers him to violate the Constitution. In a projection confession, he describes this precisely: "This is a country founded on basic freedoms, including freedom of religion...our Constitution clear."

Obama continues, "And if we ever abandon those values [which is what he's doing], we would not only make it a lot easier to radicalize people here and around the world, but we would have betrayed the very things we are trying to protect." Obama has helped radicalize Islamic terrorists and betrayed America as a Stockholm Syndrome illegal president. He alludes plainly to how easy the political class made it on him to hide—ignoring his illegality.

It's also obvious how easily he rationalized his overt lie knowing he was running as an illegal presidency. He still can't see its importance thinking he was entitled to it and blind to his programmed Stockholm Syndrome.

Consciously he insists the radical Islamists to which he's blind are protected by the rule of law—"The pluralism and the openness, our rule of law, our civil liberties, the very things that make this country great." Unconsciously he admits to doing the exact opposite revealing just how distorted is his Stockholm Syndrome mind.

He so glibly violates the rule of law it doesn't register in his conscious mind.

As a true believer in "pluralism" and political correctness he's preoccupied with reshaping civil liberties and "what makes this country great." If necessary, that means taking the law into your own hands at times.

Thinking he's inclusive and a peacemaker, unconsciously his violence runs off the charts. He's totally blind to his rule of law violations, but his unconscious sees it clearly.

He confesses that he repeatedly attacks this great country—America's exceptionalism, "The very things that make us exceptional"— per his secret instructions.

In two back-to-back denial confessions Obama admits his secret goal "and then the terrorists would have won, and we cannot let that happen. I will not let that happen." The epitome of a Stockholm Syndrome: then the terrorists win. For emphasis, Obama confesses twice that he is, in fact, letting the terrorists win, making it happen.

Obama's super-intel continues its revelations.

He confesses to the one central way he has already won as a secret Stockholm Syndrome terrorist—attacking America at its most exceptional place, most exceptional office, as an illegal president. The moment Obama violated the rule of law as an illegal president he totally capitulated to radical Islam, blind to who he was, and he completely lost his judgment. Then undercover he could continually enable radical Islam— while consciously remaining blind to his actions. Now he thinks he's protecting America while he gives it away.

Obama specifically takes us back to winning the presidency and to who else "let that happen." He's talking to Congress with more to come shortly: "You let a secret terrorist thinking the world was waiting on him illegally take office."

Obama demonstrates a thoroughly distorted mindset, thinking he can so easily violate the rule of law, the hallowed Constitution, our civil liberties and yet create a far better America and world through his grandiose globalist vision.

He can share our exceptionalism by destroying it, and share our nuclear power with our enemies. But secretly he continues to tell us precisely how to confront his presidency even at this late date—and why it's crucial. He must be stopped. He must be identified as the secret saboteur.

He provides a profile of the terrorist to aid in his identification.

Obama's self-profile: a terrorist in the White House

Obama describes the Orlando Islamist terrorist, but he's actually creating a secret picture of himself, recalling how he himself became a terrorist enabler.

Radicalized as a young man "from afar" with strong connections to Islam, he points to his own home background at a very early age.

His mind was warped by an Islamic terrorist who personally terrified him, shaping him into a secret Stockholm Syndrome extremist. Again he stresses it happened at a young age, so early that only his unconscious has detected it.

Mentioning that the terrorist was from a small cell again implies in code the home where a small number of powerful people, particularly one powerful person, radicalized him.

In turn Obama the terrorist was unconsciously "an angry, disturbed, unstable young man who became radicalized." His obvious enabling of terrorists reflects massive buried rage predictable as a result of his early abuse.

He notes a lone actor hard to detect suggesting his secret Stockholm Syndrome role— an unconscious act. On the surface he's perfectly fine. He suggests a one-man show, an illegal president yet with phenomenal power, especially hard to detect because he enjoys unprecedented political class/media support—except that his behavior shouts at us.

Remember his projection accusing Trump of being an actor in a reality show. But in fact, it's Obama who is the ultimate Stockholm Syndrome actor in the biggest reality show of all, carrying out an unimaginable charade with the perfect cover.

Secretly, like the Orlando terrorist, he pledges allegiance

to ISIS and not to America. Unconsciously Obama builds his Stockholm Syndrome identity with one vivid image after another.

Then Obama indirectly links the undercover terrorist to himself at a very crucial moment in time, *"since before I was president*—I've been clear about how extremist groups have perverted Islam to justify terrorism." Unconsciously he links his Stockholm Syndrome role to his election as president telling us that's when he became fully activated as a secret agent living out his father's "perverted Islam" programming.

Put the "two and two" code together linking "secret terrorist" and his election—the grand tell. He confesses that he carried out the ultimate Stockholm Syndrome sabotage by becoming an illegal radical Islam president.

Who would believe it? It's impossible for him to have been radicalized unless you understand just how powerful an abusive father and mother can be in a kid's life. And their abuse was reinforced when young Obama spent four formative years in Muslim Indonesia.

Don't forget, in his June speeches Obama's still talking to Donald Trump, the one man who strongly suspected Obama's illegal citizenship. Remember his projection accusing Trump of being an actor in a reality show. Obama pictures himself: the supreme Stockholm Syndrome "lone actor hard to detect" in the biggest reality show of all, carrying out an unimaginable charade.

And he almost got away with it—except for one other lone spokesman: his own super intelligence specifically confessing to his horrific deed.

Truly horrific if indeed he pulled it off. Plainly he did as he goes on to admit it compellingly in code.

Who do you think his super-intel would address specifically? The people most responsible. So Obama started with Congress to underscore how badly they dropped the ball but instructing them what they could still do about it.

Obama's parable story: examine illegal presidency now

Obama's confrontation of Congress takes us to the most powerful part of his Stockholm Syndrome story to point us where to go from here.

In code, he underscores where his Stockholm Syndrome role in America started and how he got away with it. In his speech he tells a key story related to Congress. *Think of it as a parable about himself revealing key details of his confession and undercover plan.* Stories are the hallmark of super-intel communication similar to projective tests in psychology.

In a major projection the story is about his high-level presidential appointee (Adam Szubin) whom the Senate has not yet approved for office after a long delay. The man is to play a crucial role for America in the battle with ISIS. Linking the story to himself, the man is code for Obama.

Again Obama confesses his most radical Islamist secret Stockholm Syndrome attack in the brief vignette. He states, it's "critical... the Senate confirm" this appointee. The man serves both parties and "can lead our fight against ISIS...keep our country safe." After a long delay "he still has not been given a full vote" which "is inexcusable."

"So it's time for the Senate to do its job, put our national security first" and "keep our country safe."

They must have a vote—suggesting what should have been done before his election and still can in a different way. Blatantly he's telling Congress they failed to keep our country safe as millions of American's can see.

Obama intimates that Congress has inexcusably delayed a *full vote* to approve him. Obama implies he's not really in office, confessing he's a self-appointed illegal president.

Obama's super-intel passionately declares in code that he was never fully vetted by Congress and America. His super-intel tells us, "You have an illegal president in office. That's how badly I was brainwashed, that's how self-deceptive I am."

Obama links his illegal presidency to his failure to protect

America in the war on ISIS—tying together the two severe violations of the Constitution.

His self-parable reveals his enormous vulnerability. His super-intel now instructs America what to do.

Two birth certificate deceptions

He points to two major deceptions on his part which can be investigated. First to the alleged birth certificate on record in Hawaii he refused to release. His super-intel validates that it does not exist. In other words, he admits he's an illegal immigrant.

It was rumored that a state of Hawaii official had claimed that a birth certificate was on file—but that statement was never actually issued. It would be contradicted by Obama who would not release any records. And if Hillary Clinton as Secretary of State can lie about her email records in order to become president, might not a state official in Hawaii favorable to Obama lie on his behalf? Meanwhile, a key government records department employee in Hawaii testified in a signed affidavit that no birth certificate existed. So we have a case of the Obama "non-birth certificate" birth certificate.

The only birth certificate Obama provided prior to his presidency was the unofficial short-form version he posted online, the certificate of birth also judged later to likely be a phony. Such a certificate can easily be obtained by a family member or anyone who simply claims to have witnessed the birth.

For the record his 18-year-old mother did not meet age requirements to have him declared an American citizen despite his foreign birth.

She would have been desperately motivated to fraudulently obtain a short-form certificate of birth with her family's help in Hawaii (which automatically produced a newspaper announcement). Obama's Kenyan father would have had primary custody rights with a foreign birth.

Secondly Obama validates that the birth certificate he produced in 2011 was a forgery.

The critical idea of Congress confirming his qualifications for office fits his exact scenario in code. Congress did not originally "take a vote" on Obama in 2008 as a presidential candidate. They ignored the questions about Obama's citizenship. They accepted the superficial validation of his legal citizenship he provided. The Constitution deserved far more. Unconsciously he brings us back to the birth certificate which he originally refused to release.

He confesses that he was entitled to the presidency without approval of Congress outside the Constitution—just as in his story he demanded his appointee be approved. Here Obama's great unconscious confesses in 2008 that he knew there was no long-form authentic birth certificate in Hawaii to release.

He has always seen himself as entitled to disobey the Constitution.

Under pressure in 2011 he finally produced the alleged long-awaited birth certificate. Forensic experts concluded it was almost certainly a phony, but this second crucial matter about his birth certificate was ignored by Congress. An extensive investigation by a panel of forensic experts led by noted Maricopa County, Arizona Sheriff Joe Arpaio provided extensive documentation pointing to a fraudulently created document.

The birth certificate was the hottest political potato in history, completely untouchable—until now. Obama unconsciously continues to urge that he be investigated—that's just how badly he wants to be a free man.

Obama points again to this stunning reality. *To this date no governing authority has seen the birth certificate—only an online copy he produced. No governing authority has shown the slightest interest in verifying its authenticity.*

51

Obama: Congress must demand Hawaii records showing no birth certificate exists

Not only could Congress at any time investigate the 2011 birth certificate, Obama wants them to take it a step further and specifically instructs them how. They could demand Hawaii release Obama's state records and determine if indeed it existed at all. *In his gun control speech earlier this year, Obama called in code for exactly that. He urged Congress to demand state records on dangerous gun sellers who sell weapons illegally, who do violence to America.* He was alluding to his assault on the United States Constitution as an illegal president lacking a birth certificate who now illegally provides weapons to Iran.

The bottom line: Obama has provided us with super-intel proof that he's a Stockholm Syndrome president, an illegal president. He's urging us to pursue the truth. There is an airtight case against him.

He adds one last warning—America's future depends on this matter.

In "parable code" Obama tells us the approval or non-approval of this political appointee—himself—is still crucial to national security. "So it's time for the Senate to do its job, put our national security first" and repeats "keep our country safe." Now!

He reminds Congress that it egregiously allowed an illegal president in office who has secretly been attacking America's national security for nearly eight years. Not only could it have all been prevented, Obama's warning us the damage will continue unless they act now. They must reset the rule of law. That's how they keep America safe.

Read Obama's confession, "I made America unsafe"— exactly what a Stockholm Syndrome president is supposed to do. Read it even more clearly, "I'm making America unsafe every day." As long as Obama continues outside the law he uproots it daily. His lawless decisions have made us progressively unsafe. Unsafe from terrorists and unsafe on our streets from his refusal to enforce the rule of law encouraging citizens to violate it.

Truly he's the "anti-law enforcement" president. The rule of law sets the boundaries of safety and how we judge reality. Either we're living within it or we're not. But Obama has fostered the belief among millions they can live outside the law making up their own reality as he does. That's what happens to Stockholm Syndrome victims—the rule of law goes so they can survive. But Obama's super-intel knows America can't survive outside the reality of a safe society.

Obama's telling Congress it must vet him now—take a vote—and identify him a as an illegal president. His refusal to call radical Islam terrorists by name is a proxy message for Congress: you refuse to identify me as a secret radical Islamist. Time to call me by name.

Of course Congress will not take these recommended actions on its own. Can anyone imagine that our representatives would ever take responsibility for their shabby treatment of the citizens by enabling Obama's destruction of the rule of law?

But Obama still has a super-intel plan. He continues to talk to Congress, but he's really talking to the boss of Congress—the American people. Only the people have what it takes to get the job done.

As George Washington warned in his farewell address, none of the three branches can ultimately hold themselves accountable. If the people don't do it, there will be no accountability.

3

OBAMA'S DEEP DOWN COMMON-SENSE PLAN

Meaningful way to protect America—enforce the rule of law

Obama's super-intel adamantly repeats its guidance about what America should do now.

Obama continues talking to Congress in code, emphasizing how they must deal with his illegal presidency. In projection mode he comments on American "homegrown terrorists" in San Bernardino and Orlando alluding now to his secret sabotaging role. Again we must identify Obama as the brainwashed terrorist among us.

He describes the *"meaningful way"* to protect Americans from them—read him. Plainly, leaders have not taken meaningful actions to control him.

He suggests, "Help law enforcement …make it harder on people who want to kill Americans to get their hands on weapons of war."

Obama had his Stockholm Syndrome instructions to enable radical Islam to wage war against America. The weapon that Obama got his hands on was the presidency. Millions of Americans can testify how he's used the presidency to enable violence to this country in countless ways.

Obama continually focuses on gun control confessing he's the Stockholm Syndrome gunslinger who needs controlling.

How do we do it: "Make it harder on people"—read him—to have his weapon of violence. Help law enforcement enforce the laws. He implies that Congress should take the illegal presidential gun out of his hands.

He elaborates on "common-sense steps" that could "reduce gun violence…[control] somebody who intends to do other people harm (his Stockholm Syndrome again)." Give the government agency in charge "the resources they need to enforce the gun laws that we already have." In other words, Congress should be urged to do the job it never did: enforce the Constitution. Use the power that says nobody's above the rule of law.

He goes on, "People with possible ties to terrorism"— another Stockholm Syndrome image—are not allowed on a plane and shouldn't have a weapon. Obama's super-intel conjures up ideas that he should not be allowed on Air Force One and that he should not have the weapon of the presidency at his disposal.

Adamantly he demands, "Enough talking…actually be tough on terrorism and stop making it easy as possible for terrorists to buy…assault weapons." He harkens back to how easily Congress had accepted his illegal presidency—and his enabling of terrorists. Obama's super-intel continues desperately pleading to be stopped.

Notice his key plan: common sense. How badly it's missing among the entire political class. Only the people and Donald Trump have applied common sense to Obama's enormous violation. At this late date, only the people can bring common-sense pressure on the government. Obama reveals Jesus' primary method of identifying key blind spots: look for unconscious projections—the huge log in the eye. In one projection after another, one Stockholm Syndrome image after another, Obama has spelled out his secret story.

Read the enabling code: he's the homegrown terrorist sitting on the throne of his illegal presidency. Over and over Obama confirms his central destructive pattern: violation of the rule of law while enabling others to do so.

He insists: take the gun of an illegal, destructive presidency out of his hands. His obsessive focus on gun control represents one massive projection—a powerful message that *he's the gun we need to control.*

Why Obama is telling us this now

He knows he has done incalculable harm to America. Unless we repair the damage and bring him to justice, his injustice will continue to be magnified.

Obama's also warning us now because his assaults on America and the rule of law will continue unabated. He intends to be the most powerful ex-president imaginable. He's predicting the coming hurricane, *"Obama's secret third-term plans: he'll become the most disruptive former president in history."* He's not really leaving office. Not an illegal third term but a perfectly legal third term as people have always feared. He has been planning this move all along.

This is why we must understand precisely why Obama is again confessing his illegal presidency. Ladies and gentlemen, the Obama Stockholm Syndrome terror continues. But there is a way out. He's warning us his future unabated actions can be prevented. He knows now is the perfect time to stop him. In fact, it's now or never.

Obama presidential oath story

To appreciate how important his Stockholm Syndrome confession is we look back to his severe warning everyone missed on the day he took office. In his 2009 inaugural address Obama unconsciously admitted he was a Stockholm Syndrome president and that he would secretly wage war against America from day one.

We must appreciate the terror of his unconscious Stockholm Syndrome that controlled him. We will never find a more powerful description.

When Obama became president, with all that power now suddenly his, he was facing radical Islam, a living, breathing reality in a new terrifying way. It was as if his abusive father—his chief programmer—had suddenly been reincarnated standing there next to him.

As president Obama symbolized America. He had control of all of the nation's political and economic influence…and weapons. But with all that power he was secretly Patty Hearst in the bank surrounded by persecutors with his instructions you better not dare use it in any major way against us. Because in his programmed mind his terrorists were constantly pointing the guns at him.

At that terrifying moment Obama was looking dead on at both his father and his father surrogate, radical Islam. All his fears came bubbling back from deep down inside—they were pointing guns at him. They were poised to destroy him.

This was the Stockholm Syndrome moment his persecutors had groomed him for and, as Patty Hearst had learned, any false move meant sudden death.

The opening line in Obama's inauguration speech in 2008 said it all, *"America is now at war with a far-reaching network of violence and hatred."*

Decode his projection: deep down in his post-traumatic mind, *"Obama is now at war with a far-reaching network of violence and hatred."* He could still clearly see his radical Islamic father with utter hatred for Obama gleaming in his eye, ready to act upon it. He visualized him encouraging his far-reaching Islamist terrorist network to act upon it. In the back of Obama's mind, wherever he went, whatever situation he experienced, he faced this same father anew every day in security briefings and beyond.

Obama was now at war to save his life—a Stockholm Syndrome war.

His only hope as president was to be the best, most secret Stockholm Syndrome victim in history. Self protectively he would secretly wage war against America with his father's violence and hatred. He'd attack America in the most violent way he secretly could. He simply made sure that Islam could have its way whenever he could bring it about which was often. Indeed America was *"now at war with a far-reaching network of violence and hatred"* that reached all the way to the White House.

Like Patty Hearst, Obama had his instructions: rob America. First, rob America of her national security, then capitulate to radical Islam.

No wonder he would blatantly ignore all his military advisors and pull American forces out of Iraq allowing ISIS free reign. No wonder he would fall all over himself in gift wrapping a nuclear deal for terrorist Iran.

This is why we must understand what's coming up in his unofficial third term. He will continue as a Stockholm Syndrome ex-president. America will still be at war as long as he has presidential credibility. His attacks will never let up. He will push for his Iran deal beyond belief and do everything to prevent it being blocked.

Obama's third-term plans

Obama will be out of office in a few months. Plain and simple he's not going away. He's planning on remaining in the political arena as a grand and glorious ex-president. His plan to live in Washington, D.C. carries the blatant message that he will be extremely politically active—constantly available to the media.

He will make more television appearances than any ex-president ever. He will deliver speeches far and wide. He will be proclaimed an American hero by the media exerting enormous control over the Democratic Party, a fixture at every party convention. If we thought the media fawned over him now, just wait. His potential to be even more divisive will escalate. As he warned, supposedly jokingly, halfway through his second term, "No telling what I might do. I feel like a bear out of a cage."

Indeed, he's been a secret bear on the loose in America especially over the last two years. *He has disguised his attacks through his major tactic: enabling.*

Since 2014 his escalating disruptive tactics have produced unsafe communities, racial division, blacks increasingly viewing themselves as victims, violence directed at police, disrespect for the legal process and the rule of law. Meanwhile, terrorism now plagues America even as the country suffers with an ongoing sluggish economy. Obama helmed a disastrous Iran nuclear deal while remaining blind to the worldwide rise in terrorism. His immigration policies— illegal and legal-- encouraged secret terrorists within the U.S.

All of these enabling actions were linked—either overtly or indirectly—to violating the rule of law.

As an ex-president, Obama will continue driving his divisive agenda at every turn as a programmed Stockholm Syndrome victim who was also finely tuned by leftist Saul Alinsky. And he knows it. Obama will remain a smoothly disguised dangerous bear continuing his primary cover-up strategy: enabling the continued destruction of the rule of law.

He will keep fighting America's longstanding moral compass at every turn. Yet deep down, because of his own moral compass guaranteeing him life, liberty and the pursuit of happiness, Obama yearns to be free of his Stockholm Syndrome victim role.

Ship America

Obama's great unconscious mind—his super-intel— understands the crisis he has created better than anyone.

He knows America is at a turning point. Its very existence at stake—its foundation in the rule of law severely damaged because of a lack of courage among politicians.

Eight years ago, in a very real way, Ship America suffered a devastating torpedo blast to its hull. A gaping hole still exists, and the ship's taking on water. The ship can never stay afloat, never protect its own shores, never continue its shipments of freedom and protection around the world unless that hole is repaired. But the torpedo struck under the water line. Only those ship builders and repairers who can see it and get to it, can fix it. The repair material must be as strong as the original hull—rule of law material.

Obama's super-intel is begging, "Stop me." He knows deep down that it's now or never that America face the damage he's done—and will continue to do.

He knows full well that, if elected, Democrat Hillary Clinton will continue her assault on America's rule of law foundation. She will be the second president in a row to follow the teachings of Saul Alinsky. She will lie at every turn, seeking her self-interest above all, continue Obama's politically correct agenda, and his radical destruction of America's foundations. She'll continue flaunting the rule of law, establish radical immigration policies, encourage a destructive economy, continue Obama's ill-advised policies in Iran, and fail to stop terrorism. *The gaping hole in Ship America will only grow larger, as we sorely lack enough rule of law material in the ship to keep us afloat.*

Key journalist repeats Obama warning—most important issue ever

Several influential journalists charged with holding both political parties accountable have unconsciously picked up on their own blind spots regarding Obama's illegal presidency. Like Obama, like all of us, they all possess a quick-read super intelligence that sees the real truth in his story.

In a later chapter we will see these journalists confess that they know unconsciously the exact story Obama tells. They intuit who Obama actually is and the harm he continues to do to our country. Just as Congress missed the story, these reporters collectively agree unconsciously they missed it too, as a result of political bias. They utterly failed to do their job—and still do projecting Obama's failures onto others especially Trump.

A prominent journalist highlighted precisely what Obama has done most basically to America--and resonates with Obama's warning.

Recently Roger L. Simon—founder of pjmedia.com—writing about the 2016 election underscored the crucial matter of the rule of law involving the investigation into Hillary Clinton's emails as Secretary of State. Simon declares that the rule of law is the most important issue in any election.

But unconsciously he was looking back to Obama's 2008 election, making several crucial links to Obama.

"This is far and away the most important issue of the election," he said. "All others pale compared to it."

Obama's violation of the rule of law had sent America into a tailspin, violating its very foundation. There's only one way to resolve the matter and halt the erosion—re-establish the foundation created by the rule of law—hold him accountable to it. Exactly as Obama's super intelligence pleaded.

Blood on his hands

Every guilty criminal unconsciously wants to be stopped. Deep down Obama wants to be stopped. He has blood on his hands and knows it. Look at ISIS, look at the Middle East. It's on him. With Iran waiting in the wings, their planes are nearly loaded with the nuclear weapons which were Obama's gift to that notoriously brutal Islamic state.

Read his January 2016 warning that "climate change is the

greatest threat to the world." Consider this in light of his startling Stockholm Syndrome confession. Decode the message by simply adding one word, "*nuclear* climate change is the world's greatest threat."

His secret identity changed the entire world. *He's the secret climate changer—the biggest danger to the world.* Fits hand-in-glove, doesn't it? And millions of Americans see it, but too many in Congress remain controlled by beltway blindness and a politically correct president playing his only ace to the hilt.

Action Obama now recommends

His super-intel presents one abiding message: nobody's above the rule of law.

Remember not one congressional official has examined Obama's alleged birth certificate, the one he finally produced under duress in 2011 after years of great resistance—the only Obama birth certificate anyone has ever seen.

Here are his claims for an authenticated legal presidency: the Democratic Party, his short-form "certificate of live birth" (also judged fraudulent by document examiners), the state of Hawaii's certification and two newspaper birth announcements easily obtainable as was the short certificate of live birth.

This ignores Obama refusing to release all records from grade school on up: passport, college registration, scholarship applications (revealing any claims of foreign birth), academic records including law school and all his medical records. This matched his presidency which even the liberal media called the most secretive and opaque in history—after he claimed it would be the most open.

Obama's recommendation is now plain. Congress should investigate his birth certificate on two fronts. First they should pass legislation instructing the state of Hawaii to release his long-form birth certificate. Almost certainly it does not exist which would automatically prove the 2011 alleged birth certificate was indeed a forgery.

At the same time Congress should convene an official forensic document committee to examine his 2011 birth certificate as to authenticity.

Obama has left evidence in two major ways. Refusing to release his birth certificate in 2008 and then producing one under pressure in 2011. Both matters are the eight-billion-pound gorilla in America's living room waiting to be investigated. Will our great nation's eventual fall be the result of a refusal to look at the evidence?

Of course Congress on its own will never pursue Obama unconscious recommendation. Can anyone imagine they would ever take responsibility for their shabby treatment of the citizens and enabling Obama's destruction of the rule of law?

Yet Barack Obama has revealed two major weaknesses under pressure from two major sources. First in 2009 World Net Daily—a news and opinion website—created a national billboard campaign, "Where's the Birth Certificate?" In 2011, the site published Jerome's Corsi's book under the same title. The book was a pre-release New York Times bestseller with a May publication date. Two weeks before Corsi's book came out, Obama surprised everyone by producing an alleged birth certificate.

Obama suggests another campaign, "Examine the Birth Certificate"—"Nobody Above the Rule of Law," run by the citizens who demand Congress take this action. The millions of citizens outside the beltway who never had a voice and strongly believe Obama's an illegal president. Imagine a far larger campaign than ever before. The people have the power, not Congress.

They would be following Obama's super-intel instructions loud and clear, "So it's time for the [Congress] to do its job, put our national security first" and "keep our country safe."

Demand they do it. As a Stockholm Syndrome ex-president he will continue to make America progressively unsafe.

Trump, the leader America needs

But the people need a visionary leader. How do you stop a smooth Stockholm Syndrome president who enjoys enormous cover with his surface popularity? A two-term president who has successfully, a la Alinsky, "bored from within" as a true patriot-in-disguise enabling radical Islam every step of the way.

Obama's super-intel gives them the vision—and it points to the leader who has embraced it this far, the only man in America who actively pursued it.

Enter Donald Trump who recently exposed Obama's other great weakness—his refusal to protect America's national security. Telling Obama something sinister's afoot. Because Obama's not protecting us from radical Islam, Trump advised him to simply leave office.

Obama confirms that he feels Donald Trump's relentless pressure. The one man to whom Obama confessed his Stockholm Syndrome role—the one man who might have the courage to see an investigation through about Obama's birth certificate. If elected, Trump the president would have plenty of opportunity to force a probe. Yet even if he lost, Trump might become more determined than ever to seek the truth about Obama.

Trump's the one person who has consistently stood up to Obama's illegal presidency. This is why Obama confessed to him and America— as much as he fears it, he *wants* to be stopped.

Obama has been secretly confessing to Trump since 2011. At the White House Correspondent's annual dinner in April 2011 Obama mocked Trump for calling him an illegal president. Between the lines Obama's sarcastic humor spoke volumes. He, praised Trump for his "credentials and breadth of experience" suggesting Trump demonstrated authority and experience in his pursuit of Obama's real birth certificate.

Obama continued to jokingly praise him, "job well-handled sir"—once more suggesting the message, "you're on the right track." Trump showed he could take an insult from Obama—who insulted no one around this issue as he did Trump.

Three weeks later while in England, Obama responded to a business discussion, "I know a good investor—Donald Trump." Yet another biting joke, but he implied secretly "invest in Trump," while simultaneously delivering an even deeper unconscious message, "Trump is a good investigator."

In 2014 Trump stuck to his guns offered to make a $50 million contribution to Obama's favorite charity if he would release his birth certificates.

This is why now in code Obama calls him America's symbolic national security director. Obama's national security breech was the biggest in American history. Obama made a frontal assault on the rule of law, the Constitution and the foundation of the nation.

Donald Trump—the man who William F. Buckley proclaimed would never do anything really important for America—has unconsciously uncovered the biggest cover-up in American history. Given the stakes now in our world with the secret sabotage, Obama, having turned nuclear bombs over to terrorist nations, Trump has made an enormous contribution. He prompted Obama's huge tell. To finally bring Obama to justice would be one of the most heroic acts in our history.

As mentioned back in 2011 Obama could see Trump's potential presidential capabilities. In this current speech he puts Trump down as the Republican nominee because he's scared of him. Obama followed up later declaring Trump "is unfit to be president." Read through his denial to hear him declare, "Trump is indeed fit to be president." See Obama's projection also, *he's* the one unfit to be president. Beyond that Trump has smoked out noted Obama enablers. He provoked them into a super-intel confession, confirming the big lie perpetrated on the American people. In a real way he has done something only a true leader could do.

Companions in denial urge Trump on

Unconsciously prominent media supporters of Obama have continually confessed to his illegal presidency in their denial. They cannot drop the subject, continuing to berate "birthers," especially Trump.

CNN commentator Anderson Cooper immediately pressured Trump the presidential candidate to renounce his "birther ways." Trump countered that Hillary Clinton previously questioned Obama's birth place.

In another interview CNN's Wolf Blitzer tried to hotbox Trump into a birther retreat. Frustrated when he couldn't budge him, Blitzer declared, "We must do something about protecting Obama's legacy." Read Blitzer's terrifying projection—he must protect his own legacy and that of his colleagues like Cooper whose legacy would take a hit from which they would never recover if the truth came out. Indirectly, controlled by their buried guilt, they were pushing Trump to pursue the matter by challenging him—right up his alley.

Not long after this in 2016 Michelle Obama made several speeches bemoaning how many birthers still did not believe Obama's presidency was legitimate—another projection confession that she knows the truth better than anyone. But she joins the growing crowd whose guilt prompts the foolish strategy: we will hammer you into submission to our will. In so doing, they keep alive the truth they've so diligently covered up. We will examine her super-intel confession in a brief chapter later.

Trump's instincts

As a brilliant builder Trump possesses natural instincts which made him especially attuned to Obama's violation of America. From an early age he worked on construction jobs with his father. It starts with laying the foundation that the whole structure rests on. Better than anyone, a New York builder knows how deep building foundations go—multiple stories below ground. Deep, deep foundations are in your bones.

He could quick-read Obama attacking America's basic foundations in growing and repeated ways. The borders, the economy, businesses, national security and most of all the rule of law.

From his career Trump gained an acute awareness of frameworks and boundaries. He could see that Obama never adhered to boundaries, always modifying frameworks.

Intuitively Trump could spot a person with a weak foundation. Despite Donald Trump's rough edges, he has a highly developed intuition—it's just natural to him.

Then there was 9/11. It had a unique meaning for Trump. He saw the Twin Towers fall, knew who built them just like the towers he built. Symbolically he was the New York skyline more than any builder in Manhattan. When the radical Islamist terrorists attacked on 9/11, they attacked him. It was very personal. He never forgot.

He also saw Obama tearing down the U.S. military. As the leading cadet officer at the New York Military School he attended as a teenager, Trump had developed a special sense of the military's crucial role. The military was forever a part of him, too.

Clarifying the vision—the hope for America

Amidst his Stockholm Syndrome destruction, Obama has decreed that we stop him. He has chastised the political class which has enabled him. He has repeatedly confessed he should leave office—for good. Imagine the possibilities. If we follow Obama's secret vison, the man who did such unimaginable injustice to America now brings himself to justice. Plain and simple he is shown to be an illegal immigrant, not an American citizen. By law, immigrants must register as such for three years before applying for citizenship.

We recall Richard Nixon leaving office in shame in 1974. That dramatic moment would pale in comparison if Obama—according to the rule of law, according to the presidential oath he took with his hand on the Bible—were declared an illegal president. It would be a sad day for America, a day of pathos but in its own way a great day as the country declares once and for all that *nobody—nobody—nobody—is above the rule of law.*

Prominent Obama supporters in the media give the same super-intel guidance Obama did, deep down quick-reading his repeated secret confessions all along. They make the identical recommendations he does while consciously rejecting them.

A well-known liberal columnist confessed subconsciously that the Democratic Party is only one phony Obama birth certificate identification away from collapse—and that it needed cleansing of its monstrous destruction of the rule of law. We will explore that story and other columnists who agree with him deep down in the next chapter.

Liberal media members aren't the only journalists who feel deep guilt over their failure to report the truth about Obama. The conservatives have their share of misguided journalists who scapegoat Trump because of their own failure to investigate Obama's legal claims to the presidency. And now Trump's position as a presidential candidate prompts powerful hidden guilt in them.

But Obama finally would be free and accountable. Life is short. He wants accountability, he must have it to be true to himself. To finally declare himself free of his severe abuse from his father.

America's test

Could our society ever stand such a test of courage? A delayed legal investigation of Obama's presidency? Of course there would be rampant protests such as we've never imagined.

Prior to Obama's election, a Republican member of Congress said that if they had challenged his birthplace there would be blood in the streets.

Given Obama's enabling of violence in our society, would the protests spill over into violence? Many followers would think people are trying to take something earned away from Obama playing the expected race card. Secretly terrified of the answer to the basic question, "Did he legally earn—qualify for—the presidency?" Or of its corollary question, "Did he earn the right to destroy the rule of law?"

We can expect the usual politically correct Democrat supporters to insist that asking for Obama's 2011 birth certificate to be authenticated is racist. The same way they bullied their way past any legal verification in 2008 and again in 2011.

We know how Martin Luther King Jr. would answer the question in a heartbeat: the rule of law is colorblind and prevails above all else. We must constantly stand up to injustice.

The need to investigate Obama is now. It must be done before the streets get any more out of order, before radical protest groups who feel entitled to break the rule of law get any more expressive.

Obama's severe warning to America suggests, "Investigate me now, while you still can."

Can we face the test of truth for our great nation? It's a stunningly clear test. Rule of law or bust? And if we remain in avoidant denial we are busted as we break up our foundation piece by piece. Understand the rule of law is really the rule of life.

But Obama implies unknowingly that he planned the great test as his own. Would he finally stand up for his destroyed foundation and find the solid rule of natural law, the foundation his father stole from him even before he was born?

If we take the measure of our nation, the country we're letting slip through our fingers, and stand up to the test facing us, we fight for our very foundation in the grand tradition of our founders. The very founders Obama pointed to in his 2008 inauguration speech, secretly searching for a real father. It was as if he had to become "the father of our country" to find one.

Not long ago, Thomas Sowell wrote a column entitled, "Fate of any society rests in ideas of intellectuals." We all have an intelligence far beyond what we realize. Obama's super intelligence has spoken. His deeper ideas show us our fate depending upon which road we take. Understanding the rule of law or failing to.

If Trump accepts this mission—which is his test too—he will lead the people to reclaim the rule of law. Win or lose the presidency, Trump will lead us to stand up to eight years of Stockholm Syndrome presidential abuse with four more on the way if Clinton wins.

Win or lose, Trump is well-positioned to declare enough is enough.

Summary of Obama's birth certificate issue and questions of legal presidency

Barack Hussein Obama was reportedly born on August 4, 1961, in Hawaii.

He refused to release his official birth certificate from the Hawaii Department of Health, spending millions of dollars to fight legal demands for records made prior to and after his election.

Under pressure from a best-selling book in 2011 (*Where's The Birth Certificate?*), Obama finally produced an alleged birth certificate after reportedly sending an envoy to Hawaii. It was posted online.

Reputable document examiners declared the birth certificate a likely phony. It also contained multiple contradictions regarding the alleged hospital of birth.

Forensic document experts who found evidence of forgery in the long-form certificate included Joseph F. Newcomer, Paul Irey, Doug Vogt and Mara Zebest, an expert in Adobe Photoshop whose report was published by American Thinker.com. Software designer Tom Harrison, a man with more than 30 years' experience in graphic design, called the birth certificate "a document far too complicated to be genuine."

No government official has ever examined it for authenticity.

Congress and the media ignored any possibility of fraud.

Prior to his election, the only certification of Obama's birth was an unofficial Certificate of Live Birth (COLB). It could be obtained by any resident of Hawaii (including a parent, relative, friend, etc.) claiming to have knowledge of a Hawaiian birth, typically those occurring at home. Anyone who was willing to go to the appropriate government office and pay the fee could get a COLB.

The COLB was reportedly released through an Obama campaign spokesman to a pro-Obama Internet site. Document examiners later found multiple discrepancies with this rough document.

A government employee in the Hawaii Department of Health records department testified that no birth certificate existed.

Two newspaper announcements in Hawaiian papers of Obama's birth reveal both obtained records from the DOH which reported births from COLB registrations. In other words any supposed witness to the birth produced the announcements.

No official records exist proving the parents were ever actually married or lived together.

Obama's mother left Hawaii within weeks of his birth. She moved to Seattle and did not return to Hawaii until his father, Obama, Sr., had earned his degree and moved away. She suggests abuse, and the father had a long history of spousal abuse in other marriages.

Evidence for a Kenyan birth include: Kenyan newspaper reports, acclaim by the Kenyan Congress and the testimony of a Kenyan step-grandmother. Additionally, Immigration and Naturalization Service records of flights into Hawaii from foreign countries were missing *only* for the week of August 1-7, 1961, when his mother may have flown back from Kenya.

No birth pictures of Obama have been released including of the mother, father or child. If a Kenyan birth occurred, a camera was likely not available.

Even if he was born in Hawaii at the time of his birth, Obama's "underage" 18-year-old mother did not meet requirements to confer on her son "natural born citizen" rights—a constitutional requirement for a president. His Kenyan-born father was not an American citizen. If Obama had actually been born in Hawaii, he would be considered a "native-born" citizen.

Obama's birth has been shrouded in secrecy.

In 2011, Donald Trump declared Obama's birth saga as "the scam of the century."

Stockholm Syndrome images in Obama's speeches

- Obama presents a compelling picture of his secret Stockholm Syndrome identity. In projection code he declares, "if someone seriously thinks." In other words, his serious super-intel describes in rich denial imagery his classic Stockholm Syndrome: "I don't know who we're fighting…confused about who our enemies are."

- Calling it a "surprise"—he speaks of the "thousands of terrorists who we've taken off the battlefield." But in reality he put thousands of terrorists *on* the battlefield enabling ISIS by taking thousands of U.S. troops off the battlefield in Iraq over the strong objections of military advisors. As a Stockholm Syndrome victim he was unconsciously programmed to see American troops as the enemy.

- He describes, "addressing larger forces *that have allowed these terrorists* to gain traction in parts of the world." In other words, as the most powerful man in the world, he admits it was he himself, a Stockholm Syndrome victim, who is the larger force continually enabling terrorists "to gain traction" worldwide.

- He asks of his refusal to identify radical Islam as our enemy, "Would it make ISIL less committed to trying to kill Americans?" In code he answers, "of course it would." Unknowingly Obama confesses that he has empowered ISIS, allowing them to kill Americans. It's easy to see—Barack Hussein Obama is the very embodiment of a Stockholm Syndrome victim secretly committed to the enemy.

- "Is there a military strategy that is served by this?" Obama confesses his secret "do-nothing" military strategy "does everything" for radical Islam.

- Another infamous Obama decision regarding radical Islam clearly fits his role as a Stockholm Syndrome victim. He even paid terrorist Iran $400 million dollars in cash as a ransom for four American prisoners—and then denied that it was a ransom.

- In a November 2015 speech, Obama presented a key denial revealing specifically how his early childhood brainwashing led to his Stockholm Syndrome with its accompanying massive denial. "Groups like ISIL cannot defeat us on the battlefield, *so they try to terrorize us at home—against soft targets, against civilians, against innocent people.* Even as we're vigilant, we cannot, and we will not, subcumb [sic] to fear. Nor can we allow fear to divide us." Obama was an innocent, soft target terrorized at home. His Islamic terrorist won with a total victory changing how a defeated Obama lived out his life from then on. His multiple denials confirm that he completely "subcumb(ed)" [sic] to fear—his slip pointing to the buried subconscious horror.

- His extremely abusive father in essence singled Obama out to carry out Stockholm Syndrome Islamic violence. Obama describes perfectly his enabling role—"complicit in violence." Obama was convinced he was "at war with an entire religion," and now totally under his father's control.

- Then he was fixated on "doing the terrorists' work for them." That's the clearest single description of his secret Stockholm Syndrome role. And he was carrying it out per instructions: keep them unidentified. Never say their name. That's why he avoids saying "radical Islam" to this day.

- In two denials Obama tells us "then the terrorists would win" insisting twice "I will not let that happen." His super-intel insists this is exactly his subconscious plan: "terrorists win."

- He reveals just how entrenched his submissive Stockholm Syndrome victim role is with five more denials indirectly linked to his "advisor father." He confesses never a "moment in my seven and a half years as president where [I] have...been able to pursue a strategy" against radical Islam. Maximum denial. That's the Stockholm Syndrome at its absolute—since the day he took office.

- In projection code Obama confesses "how dangerous...[his Stockholm Syndrome] mind-set and thinking can be"—as he secretly embraces Islam. His "loose talk and sloppiness about who exactly we're fighting, where it can lead." Who—exactly—are we fighting, indeed? He admits unconsciously that his Stockholm Syndrome thinking leaves him unbelievably sloppy about the enemy's actual identity

- Consider his reference that these embedded terrorists were U.S. citizens. *But all of these people—embedded terrorists—had a phony citizenship whose true loyalty was to radical Islam in the east.* Obama's imagery clearly points to him as a Stockholm Syndrome president whose true emotional citizenship is elsewhere, and he strongly suggests he's not an American citizen and thus an illegal president.

- Obama indirectly links the undercover terrorist to himself at a crucial moment in time, *"since before I was president*—I've been clear about how extremist groups have perverted Islam to justify terrorism." Unconsciously he's links his Stockholm Syndrome role to his election as president telling us that's when he became fully activated as a secret agent living out his father's "perverted Islam" programming. Put the "two and two" code together linking "secret terrorist" and his election—the grand tell. He confesses that he carried out the ultimate Stockholm Syndrome sabotage by becoming an illegal radical Islam president.

4

THE ROBBERY OF AMERICA

The infamous picture of Stockholm Syndrome victim Patty Hearst robbing a bank represents a perfect metaphor for Barack Obama, Stockholm Syndrome victim, although on a far grander scale. Obama is America's Patty Hearst who has robbed us of our very foundations.

Here is how his rap sheet over the last eight years should appear:

Rule of law

Most importantly of all robbed us of the nation's foundation: the rule of law. Obama's administration obeys the laws he likes (e.g., transgender rules in bathrooms and locker rooms, which has no foundation in federal statutes, since this issue is too new, as Congress hasn't written any laws about transgenders; yet Obama presses on and enforces rules that have no basis in fact). In turn, then Obama does not enforce any laws he doesn't like (e.g., catch-and-release on illegals detained at the border).

Robbed the nation of the Constitution and the rule of law as an illegal president followed up by his law-breaking illegal executive orders.

Robbed nation of its borders with massive illegal immigration and refusal to enforce immigration laws.

Continued attempts to rob the Constitution of its protections: gun laws, citizenship, and borders.

Presidency

Robbed nation of a legal president.

Robbed the presidency of a truthful America-first leader. Lied to us about Obamacare, protecting borders, cost of medical care, guilty criminals, climate change, police violence and national security.

Social order

Robbed nation of police protection and safe streets especially in the inner cities.

Robbed law enforcement of its respect and safety— including robbing several policemen of their lives.

Robbed America of increased racial harmony by repeatedly playing the race card and selecting Plural is Attorneys General who led the Justice Department to implement biased policies.

Robbed blacks of self-respect and independence fostering reverse-racism groups such as Black Lives Matter.

Robbed nation, especially blacks, of respect for the legal process by downplaying jury verdicts in the case of the killings of Trayvon Martin and Michael Brown.

National security

Robbed the nation of national security—and other nations as well—enabling ISIS, terrorists attacks, the destruction of the hard won peace in Iraq.

Robbed the world of stability in the Middle East.

Robbed Israel of national security strengthening its terrorist neighbors—and attempting to undermine Netanyahu's election.

Robbed the world of America's traditional leadership leading to far more global instability.

Robbed America of safety while strengthening our enemies: Russia, China, and especially arming Iran with nuclear weapons just around the corner.

Robbed America of military strength depleting the officer corps, failure to replenish aging navy warships, depleting our nuclear arsenal, discontinuing the anti-nuclear weapon shield in Eastern Europe and one sided agreements with Iran and Russia.

Economy

Robbed people of jobs with Obamacare and an excruciatingly slow economic recovery. The result: high unemployment or part-time employment with many leaving the work force.

Robbed the middle class by redistributing income to the poor. Food stamps have been risen to historic levels under Obama.

Robbed America's economy with rising entitlement programs, restrictive business regulations including environmental protection policies, carbon taxes and massive debt.

Robbed the U.S. of energy independence by failing to utilize our own resources. Robbed the economy by preventing use of Canada's energy with the keystone pipeline. Wasted money on green energy projects benefitting influential supporters. Robbed the coal industry almost entirely out of business

Robbed the private sector while increasing the federal bureaucracy and unionized government workers.

Health care

Robbed people of their doctors with Obamacare. Robbed an overall stable medical system with Obamacare and unsustainable increasing medical costs with less coverage. A looming crisis awaits.

Robbed the poor of independence by encouraging entitlement dependency

Moral and spiritual foundation

Continues to carry out the robbery of America's foundational natural law moral compass derived from our founders insisting laws are from God. Instead Obama insists laws are from man. Specifically, robbed the Supreme Court of its constitutional basis shifting to make rulings according to personal biases.

Removed Christian voices from the marketplace insisting they move to the margins.

Robbed America of its spiritual heritage from which the moral law is derived.

Robbed the nation of its Christian heritage with its emphasis on the laws of God in the Declaration of Independence. Instead he insisted at every turn that Muslims were foundational to America.

Inalienable right to pursuit of happiness

Robbed many millennials especially of personal peace creating a sense of panic around global warming and false climate change.

Robbed conservative organizations with unfair policies, and using the IRS to harass conservatives.

Robbed America of its exceptionalism.

Robbed America of its well-being and happiness creating an atmosphere of insecurity and fostering distrust

With his incessant attacks on America's foundations, Obama has carried out the robbery of America. Only the strongest actions by citizens can halt the grand theft and restore our country's original principles.

5

THE BIGGEST COVER-UP IN THE HISTORY OF JOURNALISM

Using their own super-intel, elite reporters see the biggest secret story in the history of America, a story which they failed to report.

They all have their eyes on Obama's egregious violation of the rule of law as an illegal president. The super intelligence never takes its eye off the central issue and central violation occurring in our collective body politic. Intuitively these reporters know they've botched their mission, and they must confess.

Still unable to fully accept their shortcomings they displaced Obama's failures onto Donald Trump, the perfect foil. But unconsciously they reveal their projections onto Trump presenting a clear picture of Obama's assault on the rule of law.

They offer a sterling picture that their super-intel is by far the brightest part of their mind. They reveal that they're enormously prone to blind spots—and as journalists sharing the identical blind spot in a powerful politically charged environment. Living out a longstanding criticism, that journalists are often "birds of a feather flocking together."

Their denial about Obama also made them blind to his Stockholm Syndrome behavior and his resulting failure to protect America and the world. Yet their brilliant super intelligence—their utterly perceptive and honest unconscious minds—guides America to pursue justice.

The Journalists

Roger L. Simon
President, pjmedia.com
pjmedia.com/diaryofamadvoter/2016/03/23/james-comey-and-loretta-lynch-hold-the-whole-country-in-their-hands/

Journalist confesses Obama illegal president—rule of law crisis

The most fundamental article was written by Roger L. Simon who insisted that the ongoing FBI investigation of former Secretary of State Hillary Clinton would determine whether the foundation of America—the rule of law ("most important issue in any election")—would remain intact.

Unconsciously Simon sees that with Obama's illegal presidency, our nation's precipitous decline is already well underway. He calls for the truth.

Does America's future rest on examining the birth certificate? Roger L. Simon says it does.

When journalists subconsciously pick up on a story which they missed, their super intelligence often tells about it with a displaced story about someone else or another situation alluding to the more important matter. It's as if they're playing a "sounds-like" journalistic game of charades.

Among the prominent journalists who picked up on the real story about Obama, this recent article stands head and shoulders above the rest leading the way to the truth.

In a stunning commentary published on March 24, 2016,

Roger L. Simon—founder of pjmedia.com—underscored the crucial matter of the rule of law involving Hillary Clinton.

He insisted the magnitude of her alleged violations of national security via unsecured emails and influence-peddling to foreign nationals went far beyond similar violations by Richard Nixon and Bill Clinton, both nearly impeached. He asserted the charges in Watergate never "even remotely approach the magnitude of crimes for which Hillary Clinton is said by many to have committed."

Unconsciously Simon suggests his concern about Hillary Clinton's presidential eligibility in 2016 represents a thinly disguised secret cover for what really happened in the 2008 election with presidential candidate Barack Obama. Place the Clinton story as a template over the 2008 Obama candidacy and we find it fits perfectly with all the specific details.

The evidence is startling that Simon's subconscious quick-read skills picked up on a far more threatening Obama story—one that he had missed and one that put America's future in jeopardy.

Stuck in the back of Simon's mind was the realization that Obama's presidency began with an enormous legal issue in which the rule of law was brazenly flaunted. It's as if Simon's super-intel shouts at the world—and himself—in a shocking déjà vu.

Unknowingly he has uncovered the most powerful secret story in the history of America.

On the surface talking about 2016, Simon said, "This is far and away the most important issue of the election. All others pale compared to it." In other words, it's the most important issue in *any* election.

How it's resolved "will affect the very backbone of our country—the rule of law. No democratic society can exist without it. No person, no matter how high, can be above it. Without the rule of law, the United States of America as we know it does not exist."

'Guilty person in the White House'

Those who care about America, he insists, want no "guilty person in the White House." Simon's blatant imagery suggests there is one there now.

But he "fears Democrats don't care." Their leaders have "no tough questions for a candidate who lied under oath" (alluding to Obama's presidential oath). He sees "journalists tip-toeing around truth" reflecting cowardice, "a presidential opponent indifferent to the truth lying that people don't care [about the rule of law]," and Democrats laughing—"on the grave of our country, now in a drastic free fall."

Unconsciously Simon saw that the question of Obama's legal citizenship was quickly swept under the rug in 2008—and with it the rule of law. Simon lists the guilty parties: both political parties, the press, the opposing candidates and the courts. In short the entire political establishment.

Simon's perceptive super-intel sees that America and its media lost their backbone by rejecting the rule of law in 2008 with the shallow vetting of Obama.

He implies that Obama was an illegal candidate—a foreign national selfishly peddling influence as the first black president. Simon suggests that Obama lied to the people about his own unique key communication—the birth certificate, a vulnerable untrustworthy document—violating the Constitution from the get-go.

Simon's super-intel urgently warns that the question has dramatically shifted. Will the rule of law be broken by a current Democratic candidate? No, the real question is has it *already* been broken by Obama. Simon implies a secret World War III is well underway, and we and the media have overlooked a surprise attack by a secret foreigner.

Simon's article then envisions a tainted president, newly inaugurated in 2017, whom half the public knows "should been indicted," and shortly new evidence emerges leading to a potential impeachment.

He declares, "It's a catastrophe for the world—an absent American leader when needed most in a time as dangerous as WW II."

Decoding Simon's super-intel imagery we find more specific details about Obama's presidency—confirming the deeper story.

At Obama's inauguration many citizens ("half the public") thought he was an illegal foreign-born president. More evidence emerged when Obama finally produced a complete birth certificate. Independent document examiners quickly determined it was almost certainly a forgery, but the media and Congress ignored the findings. The people didn't. Talk of impeachment surfaced but dissipated.

A shocking cover-up had occurred leaving an illegal president in office and the powers-that-be ignoring the entire matter while the people felt helpless.

Indeed it was a catastrophe: an absent president—and on top of that an absent leader of the free world—failing to protect us or our allies. Having enabled violence and chaos in the Middle East, Obama has become a threat to world peace The chaos he enabled is now spreading to Europe. The media refused to tell the story they should be reporting nightly, a story Simon himself still cannot consciously recognize that he failed to see.

The true Obama legacy: secret Mussolini

Simon's super-intel ends powerfully by linking this matter to Obama. He warns Obama to keep his sticky hands out of an FBI/DOJ investigation. In other words, his hands were all over the 2008 election when he ignored the Constitution by violating the rule of law. Now Obama "can forget about a legacy."

Simon's final message to Obama, "call Donald Trump Mussolini if you want but...he doesn't hold a candle to you." Obama's the dictator president who took the law into his own hands and sent America reeling toward self-destruction, just as Mussolini ruined his native Italy. The America we all thought we knew no longer exists until we restore the rule of law.

What now? Simon's super-intel guides us: no person above the law; no guilty person in the White House; the future of America depends on it.

It's too late for impeachment now, but Obama must be held accountable for what he did. In the past as a nation we thought we could get away with slavery and then segregation—violating natural law. We solved the last problem when Martin Luther King Jr. spoke for all: America must apply the same colorblind law of freedom to all and cease violating it.

Out of deep residual guilt in 2008 Americans understandably allowed the "first black president" rule to supplant the rule of law, and Obama was never fully vetted. Now we must return to the idea that nobody's above the rule of law. Many enabled Obama, but he alone must face the consequences if he deviated from the moral compass.

Simon emphasizes that rule-breaking has consequences. America's leaders are caught up in a self-sabotaging cycle. One bad decision in which they failed America—enabling Obama—leads to another "guilt begets guilt/ "deserve punishment" cycle. That's a major reason they've tolerated years of presidential abuse by Obama. Until it's made conscious, it will continue.

Simon's unconscious wisdom implies that Obama should still be independently investigated by the government. For the sake of America's future, we must face the truth.

Secretly Simon reveals how the super-intel operates in a journalist who insists on telling the truth to America and to himself. As a result it's one of the most important political articles in history.

For the record, however, Simon unconsciously predicts Obama—the continual law-breaker—will act to prevent any indictment of Hillary Clinton, if necessary. (Obama later inserted himself into the process declaring Hillary did not violate the law.)

Explains media hatred of Trump

Simon also explains the media's animus toward Donald Trump. Recall that Trump was the only prominent American who consistently accused Obama of being born in Kenya. Although he made those statements long before becoming a presidential candidate, Trump's stand demonstrated the kind of courage and leadership our country needs. It was truly a presidential moment. As a result, Trump creates enormous secret guilt in these influential reporters who failed to protect America.

Not surprisingly, several other journalists have unconsciously perceived the same thing that Simon did about Obama's egregious violation. Many of these journalists are all unknowingly furious with Trump for standing up for the rule of law in the face of an illegal president. This significantly colors their take on Trump.

Consider the scariest twist of all for them. As president, Trump could boldly launch an official investigation into the authenticity of Obama's birth certificate. Trump —no stranger to tackling big deals—could be the one person in America capable of helming such a probe. Imagine how deeply that alarms elite journalists whose failure would be completely exposed, and they'd no longer be able to escape into their secret den of denial.

David Brooks
The New York Times
http://www.nytimes.com/2016/03/18/opinion/no-not-trump-not-ever.html?&_r=0).

Brooks' secret confession: Obama is an illegal president

In a recent op-ed piece New York Times columnist David Brooks unconsciously confesses that he and his mainstream media colleagues failed to break the biggest news story in America—Barack Obama is an illegal president.

In a scathing take on Donald Trump, Brooks unknowingly reveals he has projected Obama's massive faults onto the Republican front-runner.

His descriptions of Trump fit Obama perfectly. Brooks gives clear guidance on how America should now handle this stunning crisis.

In essence Brooks is telling America a powerful secret story about the utter danger we now face. He can't face it consciously, but—although it's made unconsciously—his warning is absolutely horrifying.

Step-by-step we superimpose Brooks' descriptions of Trump onto Obama, descriptions that highlight the columnist's continual projections.

Consider that Obama—not Trump—was "epically unprepared to be president...[had] no realistic policies, no advisers, no capacity to learn." Think of Obama's unrealistic policies: rampant lawless immigration which drains the economy while allowing terrorists to infiltrate; Obamacare undermining the health industry; doubling entitlements and America's debt; sabotaging the police; green-energy fiascos, hampering industry with regulations, and refusing the pipeline—consistently ruining the economy.

Brooks continues, "His vast narcissism makes him a closed fortress. He doesn't know what he doesn't know and he's uninterested in finding out...He insults the office Abraham Lincoln once occupied by running for it with less preparation" than someone buying a sofa.

Projection confession: Obama most dishonest person in high office

Consciously Brooks thinks he's describing Trump but unconsciously he's describing Obama as "the most dishonest person to run for high office in our lifetimes."

Deep down he describes Obama's presidency as "an extraordinary mix of inaccurate claims about domestic and foreign policy."

Think of Obama's misleading statistics about full employment, his lies about Obamacare, as admitted by his own advisors, that it would lower costs and that participants could keep their own doctor. While refusing to enforce immigration laws and protect our borders, Obama has been the most racially divisive president in history.

Most of all appreciate Obama's absolute absence of a cohesive foreign policy. This included undermining peace in Iraq and turning ISIS loose to obliterate stability in the Middle East. Finally he capitulates to Iran—providing the world's leading terrorist nation with nuclear weapon-making capability.

Relentlessly, Brooks criticizes, "personal and professional boasts that rarely measure up." Consider Obama's boasts about reckless immigration being "the American way," about never being above the rule of law, about ISIS being the Jayvee team and having them contained.

Obama 'childish man' who ran for president

Brooks goes on between the lines describing Obama, "He is a childish man running for a job that requires maturity. He is an insecure boasting little boy whose desires were somehow arrested at age 12. He surrounds himself with sycophants." Unconsciously Brooks knows Obama was severely traumatized early in his life—his personality development frozen. This was extensively documented in my book *The Obama Confession: Secret Fear, Secret Fury*.

Brooks' imagery declares Obama's run for office intentionally avoiding full verification of his legality was childish. He implies the political class was equally childish and immature in not vetting him.

Then Brooks comments on the truth of Obama's election: "In…rare cases, political victors do not deserve our respect…George Wallace won elections, but to endorse those outcomes would be a moral failure." Unknowingly the writer insists Obama deserved to win neither the election nor our respect.

With his George Wallace image, Brooks suggests that Obama became president solely because of his race. He implies that America made a huge mistake by allowing race to supersede all else.

Brooks actually quotes Scripture

Brooks is so attuned to moral failure by a presidential candidate that he quotes Scripture—specifically Psalm 73—as a powerful addition to his secret story.

Consciously he describes Trump, unconsciously Obama, as Brooks looks back to 2008. He implies America now faces great danger because of having selected an immoral president.

Brooks reminds us history has a long list of such nation-sabotaging leaders temporarily rising, stretching back to biblical times.

Scripture depicts such a leader: prideful, arrogant, deceitful, secretly violent ["clothe themselves with violence"], and threatens oppression.

He covertly speaks with malice and "lays claim to heaven." The people drink it up but the success is fragile. Secretly this man and his followers are on slippery ground—because they have violated the moral laws of God.

Frighteningly Brooks invokes God's condemnation, "You cast them down to ruin. How suddenly they are destroyed."

Ever more strongly, Brooks implies Obama and the citizens have committed an egregious immoral act to do with his presidential election. Soon he will clarify the matter completely.

Brooks continually goes on about moral codes, "Worse, there are certain standards more important than one year's election. There are certain codes that if you betray them, you suffer something much worse than a political defeat.

Brooks' great unconscious super-intel declares unequivocally that America's obsession to elect "first black president" Obama took precedence over all other values and resulted in something far worse.

In so doing we betrayed our standards, our most basic code. Brooks implies clearly violating the constitution, the rule of law, and specifically the absolute rule of natural law in our hearts that insists on the truth. Clearly Brooks lives by this code and must subconsciously confess how badly he violated his conscience as a reporter.

Subliminally he has seen past his denial recognizing Obama's deceitful personality and where his destructive presidency has led.

Beyond Obama's dysfunctional presidency, Brooks sets up his punchline with three powerful super-intel message markers—the Scriptures, "our most basic code," and later the Constitution.

Trump's courage triggered Brooks' guilt

Now for Brooks' grandest projection: "Trump [that is Obama] is an affront to basic standards *of honesty, virtue and citizenship*." Suddenly Brooks is back to the most crucial issue for candidate Barack Obama in 2008—the crucial question of his legal citizenship.

And we allowed it. Very few stood up to publicly protest Obama's illegality, and one of those was Donald Trump. That created powerful unconscious guilt in Brooks causing him to scapegoat Trump—projecting onto him Obama's faults.

Brooks' thoughtprints confirm the message. He goes straight to the founders who "would have understood" the constitutional code. Unconsciously he affirms Obama's presidency is illegal, "a threat to the long and glorious experiment of American self-government...He is precisely the kind of scapegoating, promise-making, fear-driving and deceiving demagogue they feared."

Brooks' final take on the illegal Obama: "He has shredded the unspoken rules of political civility....his savage regime...is just a dog-eat-dog war of all against all."

Decoding Brooks' final projection ("No, not Trump, not ever"), he secretly shouts out, 'No, not Obama, not ever.' The man who has never been a true president.

Intuitively Brooks teaches America that daily we pay a huge price for violating the rule of law. Lies have enormous consequences—whether we're in denial about them or not.

Brooks' super-intel references the psalmist's scriptural counsel "in the face of demagogy...go the other way—make an extra effort to put on...humility, to seek a purity of heart that is stable and everlasting."

In short we must seek the truth about the demagogue Obama meaning "we go the other way"—insist on a thorough investigation we assiduously avoided about his legal citizenship even after Obama leaves office. Only then can we restore the damage that's been done.

In a thinly encoded message Brooks unconsciously confessed to missing the real Obama story and projecting onto Trump, "many in the media, especially me, did not understand...We expected Trump to fizzle...and did not listen carefully enough. For me, it's a lesson that I have to change the way I do my job if I'm going to report accurately on this country." Here Brooks also makes plain he cannot fairly evaluate Trump.

All in all, Brooks' super-intel reminds us that our imperfect conscious minds can so easily be misled by the political whims of the moment. We are all prone to blind spots underscoring why we have a constitution—and must be ever attentive to its abiding framework.

Paul Krugman
The New York Times
nytimes.com/2016/03/14/opinion/trump-is-no-
accident.html?WT.mc_id=2016-MARCH-
OUTBRAIN_AUD_DEV-0301-0331&WT.mc_ev=click&ad-
keywords=AUDDEVREMARK&_r=0

Noted reporter declares Obama 'Kenyan-born'

On March 14, New York Times columnist Paul Krugman penned a vicious attack on Republican Party members and candidates Donald Trump and Marco Rubio. In fact, his super-intel was secretly talking about Democrats and Barack Obama.

In projection code, Krugman declares that Democrats are "un-American, active traitors," whose treason went off-the-charts at a "volume of 11" during the Obama years. He describes their integral paranoid strategies of playing the victim card and obfuscating the truth through tribal manipulation. He reveals how Democrats have fundamentally broken the natural rule of law.

He then specifically identifies how Obama, enabled by his corrupt party, betrayed America. In unbelievable fashion, Krugman reveals the conspiracy of silence which Democrats have adopted regarding Obama's true identity.

Krugman's super-intel presents the greatest cover-up in America's history explaining why he must tell us despite the extent of his misguided conscious opposition. He can only tell us the "Forbidden Secret" in a projection, but tell he must because his deeper moral compass sees that the America's future rides on facing this terrible truth. Krugman underscores that only "the truth sets you free." Live a lie and our nation dies.

As a Democrat insider, Krugman subconsciously presents a stunning exposé of his party and how it has been coopted by ideologues. Despite his conscious denial, Krugman's super-intel moral compass—guided by natural law our founders insisted we live by—is compelled to get America back on track.

In so doing, Krugman follows a recent pattern among elite journalists who have intuitively picked up the truth they had all missed, the story they'd refused to report about Obama's illegal presidency.

Now for Krugman's decoded story.

Denial and projection

In a nutshell Krugman unconsciously places his scathing article on Republicans and Trump ("Trump was no accident") as a template of denial and projection over Democrats and Obama to reveal a crucial truth he had overlooked in 2008.

Keep the projection code constantly in mind: Republicans equal Democrats, Trump (or Rubio) equals Obama.

Now for the decoded version of his story. Krugman opens with "Republicans who are horrified by the rise of Donald Trump." Translated, Krugman describes Democrats who are *unconsciously* horrified by Obama's abysmal leadership which they enabled.

Deep down the columnist sees the truth about Obama in a Marco Rubio comment, "Let's dispel with this fiction that Barack Obama doesn't know what he's doing." He is "deliberately weakening the nation—reducing America's stature around world." Deep down Krugman sees the fact that Obama has weakened America and diminished her reputation worldwide—rationalizing his behavior.

Looking back, Krugman continues his fixation on Obama's 2008 presidential candidacy. He alludes to Obama as the anointed Democratic Savior. He characterizes Obama (projecting onto Rubio again) as "deliberately channeling the paranoid style in American politics." While constantly alluding to Republicans as racists, misogynists, homophobes and money-grubbers, he's actually accusing Obama and his party of those same traits.

Krugman then unconsciously confesses the truth in another stunning denial regarding Rubio's take on Obama, *"suggesting, albeit coyly, that a sitting president is a traitor."* For emphasis Krugman repeats that Obama is a traitor to America projecting the idea this time onto Trump.

Democrats are "in thrall to an unpopular ideology...if voters knew more about it," Krugman further confesses. The party, he admits, wins elections through "obfuscation, demagogy and appeals to *primitive tribalism"* controlled by leaders who play the victim card and the race card using "racial dog whistles." Krugman secretly insists Democrats are "un-American if not active traitors."

Democrats dodged the obvious truth

Now for the key projection onto Republicans decoded: "Establishment [Democrats] avoided saying in so many words that the president was a *Kenyan Islamic atheist socialist friend of terrorists."*

Unconsciously Krugman confesses Democrats dodged the obvious truth: Obama was Kenyan-born, an illegal president. He was an "atheist," a non-believer in America's Constitution, attacking the nation's very foundation, the rule of law.

Now, after eight years in office, it's obvious he's also an Islamic sympathizer, a socialist and friend of terrorists. He has sabotaged peace in Iraq, enabled the rise of ISIS, and gave Iran the atom bomb.

In super-intel code, Krugman he explained the secret story: the dominating ideology in 2008 was that Obama *had* to be president regardless of birth circumstances. No one was to question it (including Krugman) per instructions from the Democratic Party. In step, the enabling media immediately began accusing anyone who opposed it of being a racist.

Krugman figured out unconsciously exactly where Obama was born by the way he and the Democrats handled the controversial birth certificate matter—starting with Obama's blatant refusal to release it. Krugman could see the obvious. In 2011 Obama impulsively produced a birth certificate under the duress of a best-seller (*Where's The Birth Certificate?* by Jerome Corsi) and increasing pressure to release his complete Hawaiian birth record. Obama produced it on his own, reportedly sending a secret emissary to fetch it.

Another red flag waved when independent forensic document examiners hired by Sheriff Joe Arpaio of Maricopa County, Arizona, found probable cause the birth certificate proffered by the White House is actually a forgery.

But the Obama-enabling media, by now both liberal and conservative, and both political parties handled the matter the same way they had handled the rule of law matter. Under no circumstances was Obama to be vetted then or certainly not after he "so cooperatively" produced the certificate. In an unconscious conspiracy of denial, it was as if the document examiners' report did not exist.

In continued projection mode, Krugman explains his party's devious strategy: to fool voters again and again into supporting Democrats "out of their rage against Those People"—implying rigid and wealthy Republicans. The Democrat secret: rule by the power of envy and victimhood disguised as entitled rage.

As a result "the [Democratic] establishment is being destroyed by the monster it created"—by Obama's secret rage and their own." And so is the country.

All along Obama has demonstrated a blue streak of passive-aggressive fury as he attempts to bury our Constitution. From day one, Obama proclaimed himself the one man in American history who had a right to change the rule of law, the very foundation of America.

The birth certificate begged to be examined, but nobody in authority wanted to look at it.

Yet deep down Krugman, Brooks, Roger L. Simon and other elite reporters know Obama's birth and birth certificate have never been truly submitted to the scrutiny of the law.

In their unconscious desperation, the super-intel of these reporters communicated independently that America suffers a major rule of law crisis. Subconsciously, they shouted in one united chorus, "Examine the birth certificate! Rule of law or we die." That's the only way to bring America back to life and halt the death spiral.

Krugman on Trump

By overtly attacking Trump, Krugman also reveals his other side, just how much he unknowingly fears the GOP nominee. He suggests that Trump taps into the appropriate anger of American voters attacked so egregiously by Obama and the Democrats. In light of his profuse confession of Democratic Party corruption, Krugman fears voters might intuitively follow Trump. Then the Democrats would face justice for their misdeeds.

In a major denial and secret instruction, *Krugman warned Trump not to dare use the Rubio tactic of implying Obama was a foreign-born illegal president. Krugman's super-intel knows that is precisely what Trump should do*—and what's best for the country. The heart and soul of natural law insists that truth shall set you free.

Intuitively, Krugman urges Trump to investigate Obama's nativity, pointing clearly at the birth certificate. He suggests Trump is the only man who could confront Obama's illegal presidency as he did before—and now completely expose the cover-up. As president Trump would have authority over an investigation into the Obama birth matter.

Trump could bring down the entire Democrat charade. He's the one man in America who could expose Obama and the Democrats for who they have become.

6

THE NATIONAL REVIEW CONFESSES ITS FAILURE TO VET OBAMA

Ramesh Ponnuru
nationalreview.com/nrd/articles/432563/never-trump
nationalreview.com/magazine/2016-05-23-0100/donald-trump-democrats-republicans-share-blame

A conservative standard's guilt-ridden confession

The semi-monthly National Review bills itself as "America's most widely read and influential magazine and website for conservative news, commentary, and opinion," but no publication has been more antagonistic toward Donald Trump—the Republican nominee—and no publication has so continually confessed secretly to the great injustice it has done to America. The National Review prides itself as the media's leading conservative voice in the tradition of its founder, William F. Buckley Jr., but it repeatedly fails to rise to his standards.

In his March 28, 2016 article, "Never Trump." National Review senior editor Ramesh Ponnuru listed reasons conservatives should oppose the Republican nominee. From beginning to the end, his magazine piece is one massive projection highlighting his and his magazine's egregious failure as journalists.

As it happens, his scathing assessment of Trump repeatedly fits Obama perfectly.

Immediate confession he's blind to truth

At the very beginning of Ponnuru's article he makes two stunning confessions of how misguided he is. Typically, his super-intel offers him a self-correction if only he could hear it. He notes that conservative commentator Bill Bennett sees Trump as "winning fair and square," and he asks, "so why grab the nomination from him?" revealing Ponnuru's own super- intel wisdom. Repeating himself, Ponnuru also quotes radio host Rush Limbaugh who accused the GOP leadership of "trying to get Trump out of the race because they're not in charge of it."

Ponnuru's critiques of Trump, secretly of Obama, include, "even if electable, Trump "would not overcome the man's manifest unfitness for the presidency...His opponents therefore have good moral and political reasons to do what they can to keep him from winning...especially by persuading some of this supporters to leave him."

Read the unconscious confession: From the get-go there were good moral reasons—constitutional reasons—to keep Obama from the presidency as he avoided being investigated and refused to release his birth certificate and other records. The issues surrounding his birth and legality deserved serious vetting—the Constitution deserved it. The National Review should have attempted to strongly persuade its readers to totally vet Obama and reject him if he refused

Obama consistently demonstrates moral failures. He repeatedly violates the Constitution and his oath of office. He has repeatedly lied to citizens about Obamacare, immigration, protecting the laws of the land—just ask Arizona—and now he lies about protecting America's national security.

But the National Review refuses to overtly report that Barack Hussein Obama is an immoral president even though the evidence is strong that he ran as an illegal candidate. They fail to identify a major "immoral" way that Obama operates with his behavior—his extremely passive-aggressive attacks on citizens noted above. In so doing, the National Review confesses that its journalists morally failed to do their job.

As for Trump not being "politically qualified" to be president, no one was more unfit than Obama—a striking unconscious reference to his illegality. In addition, we had his inexperience, lack of accomplishments, his far left platform, his Alinsky background and his association with anti-American pastor Jeremiah Wright and former Weather Underground terrorist bomber Bill Ayers.

'Anybody but Trump' cover for 'Anybody but Obama'

As National Review leads the charge for the "anybody but Trump" campaign they suggest an unconscious guilt-ridden confession they should have led an "anybody but Obama" campaign before his 2008 election.

Recall the National Review never had the courage to campaign against Obama on their front cover—as they did with Trump devoting an entire issue (February 15, 2016) to defaming the GOP candidate. Eight years before, however, the National Review simply gave Obama a free pass.

Other unconscious projections by the National Review regarding Obama include charges Trump was anti-American and would violate "military policy and international law." Ponnuru addresses the matter of the rule of law. The writer's super-intel intuits that Obama violated our nation's rule of law by falsely claiming American citizenship.

Obama has further violated international law by enabling ISIS and undermining peace in Iraq and the Middle East costing thousands of lives. He has also violated the spirit of international law by consistently retreating from leadership which can only come from America, still the world's leading power.

Unconsciously Ponnuru pictures Obama as one who has repeatedly ignored ("violated") military advisors with his reckless foreign policy.

The National Review offers another reason to withhold support for Donald Trump: he could not stand up to Hillary Clinton's negative advertisements, a supposition that suggests another projection of their own. The magazine could not stand up to the negative message of Obama's 2008 campaign which was "You're racist if you pursue my legality, and if you don't vote for me." Now they repeat their error becoming the negative ad against Trump rather than upholding party unity.

In another projection the National Review states that Trump's poll numbers are worse than Hillary Clinton's and fears losing the election, the Senate and future damage to the Republican Party. In fact, that's exactly what their failure to stand up to an illegal president cost America in 2008: a lost election, the loss of the Senate and major damage to the GOP.

Projects Obama not prepared be president

Ponnuru criticizes Trump by associating him with the racist Ku Klux Klan, accusing him of advocating torture by our soldiers and charactering him as "not prepared" to be president. These are more Obama projections onto Trump. Obama has been the most racially divisive president in history, enabled ISIS to torture Americans and allied soldiers and was completely unprepared to be president. But Ponnuru's projection also confesses that when it came to investigating Obama, the National Review lacked character.

In one more stunning projection Ponnuru makes recommendations. He suggests reconvening a possibly contested Republican convention to nominate a new candidate at the cost of breaking the party asunder—which is exactly what the National Review did in 2008. And it's repeating the same behavior now. They're totally oblivious to how they severely wounded the party and the country, yet their super-intel knows it full well.

Another alternative—a third party candidate—would guarantee a Hillary Clinton presidency. In other words, the National Review suggests conceding the presidency to Clinton—another secret confession that they conceded the 2008 election to Obama by not investigating the obvious holes in his story.

Now, out of hidden guilt over failing America, the magazine wants to punish the nation again…and itself.

But Ponnuru's rationalization is confessional: standing up for conservative principles which they utterly failed to do in 2008.

Writer—'immigration liberalizer'—points to illegal president

In a follow-up article published two months later, Ponnuru offers more astute projection confessions. In his May 23, 2016 article entitled, "Who Caused Trump?"—Ponnuru suggested that if Trump loses, his supporters will say anti-Trump Republicans had caused it. He mentions, "elected Republicans [who]…decided not to get involved in the race" alluding to the National Review's own unconscious lack of participation and active undermining. He notes that some say "Trump's rise is evidence of a deep pathology among movement conservatives"—a brutal self-analysis of the National Review's failure to investigate the illegal presidency of Obama.

Most poignantly, he attributes open immigration policies among conservatives for creating "restrictionists" who backed Trump "getting voters worked up over immigration." He added, "immigration liberalizers tried to create a consensus in the party that was a poor fit for its voters." Ponnuru's super-intel is actually pointing to *immigration liberalizers* such as the National Review which indulgently allowed an illegal immigrant to take office and tried unsuccessfully to convince conservatives he was a legal president.

Ponnuru acknowledges that some aspects of conservatives supporting Trump "are real...we have come to reward the expression of anger and resentment more than the mastery of public policy." A blatant unconscious confession that the National Review and Ponnuru himself are angry and resentful that Trump mastered the public policy of identifying and publicly decrying an illegal president when they failed so egregiously. That suffocating guilt is what drives the magazine to so boldly scapegoat Trump.

In a final stunning projection, Ponnuru tells how skepticism of the press "has made conservatives more prone to falling for lies...told by people who are or claim to be on our side. It has made us more credulous rather than less." The National Review, like all of inside-the-beltway folks, fell for the lie of a legal Obama presidency. Ponnuru is a Beltway insider based in Washington, D.C., and he and his colleagues are particularly vulnerable to the politically correct pressure of the media all around them. In short they were totally gullible and lost all their protective skepticism. They lost their ability to be truly investigative reporters. That flaw continues in their coverage of both Obama and Trump.

Enabling Obama, scapegoating Trump

The National Review has confirmed, between the lines, that it also missed the crucial story of allowing an illegal president Obama to take office for eight horrific years. The magazine's editors are now scapegoating Trump, the people's choice, because of their guilt—incessantly projecting onto Trump all of Obama's failures. Instead of admitting their inadequate journalism and calling for a new vetting of Obama, they double down on their error. They are again punishing the

Republican Party. They have failed entirely to grasp the destructiveness of an illegal president—overlooked the great damage Obama has done to our foundations. They are a living breathing example of the blindness of the political class which has led to overt violations of conservative principle.

They have totally ignored the peoples' call for a total outsider to attempt to clean up the mess. Millions of citizens are aware of Obama's illegality and intuitively know Trump is the one man who could do something about the damage that continues. The people understand the conservative media and the conservative Congress have failed to stand up to Obama and his politically correct agenda.

The National Review has demonstrated its highly overvalued opinion of their writers' and editors' collective conscious minds which remain so vulnerable to major blind spots especially in the City of Beltway Blindness.

Various comments in the National Review 'Against Trump' issue of February 15, 2016:

William Kristol

"William F. Buckley Jr. proclaimed, in the founding statement of this journal, that conservatism "stands athwart history, yelling Stop, at a time when no one is inclined to do so, or to have much patience with those who urge it. Hasn't Donald Trump always been a man inclined to go along—indeed impatiently to get along—with history?"

We decode Kristol's stunning projection confession. The National Review and other conservative leaders failed to yell "Stop" when Obama was running roughshod over the bedrock Constitution and continues to do so. Kristol and his colleagues thus have no patience with Trump who was the one leader who declined to go along with history—and endorse/enable Obama's illegal presidency. Yet deep down Kristol sees the truth as do the rest of the writers.

Edwin Meese (referring to the Republican primary)

*"Questionable assertions that an opponent is not eligible to run.....*or that another cannot be elected...or another lacks enthusiasm are a poor substitute for addressing the real issues...strengthening national security, eliminating corruption, and improving the lives of all Americans.

"At a time when the nation is suffering under one of the most divisive and incompetent presidents in history, our people need positive, unifying leadership, not negative, destructive political rhetoric."

His projection confession decoded: Meese's super-intel identifies the crucial issue about Obama's presidency—his utter corruption, "not eligible to run." America paid an inordinate price in national security and the nation suffered under the worst president in our history. Only Trump has identified this terrible assault suggesting he's the only candidate who can unify America and control the Democrats' destructive rhetoric.

Katie Pavlich

"Conservatives have a serious decision to make. Do we truly believe in our long-held principles and insist that politicians have records demonstrating fealty to them? Or are we willing to throw these principles away because an entertainer who has been a liberal Democrat for decades says some of the right things? In short, do our principles still matter? A vote for Trump [read Obama in 2008] indicates the answer is 'No.'"

Pavlich's super-intel admits the far-left wing Obama had no record of abiding by American principles such as openness about his records and birthplace. The conservatives threw their principles away in 2008 over the entertainer, Obama, who so loves making television appearances, and his minions who said the right thing.

Dana Loesch

"Just a few years ago, I, along with many others, was receiving threats for promoting conservative policies and conservative principles—neither of which Donald Trump seems to care about. Yet he's leading. Popularity over principle—is this the New Right?"

Read through Loesch's denial. In a real sense Trump cared more about conservative principles in 2011 than any other candidate. He bravely proclaimed that America had suffered a broadside attack on its rule of law foundation with an illegal president about whom the conservative political class was in denial. How can any of these elite Republican insiders trust themselves to fairly evaluate Trump's candidacy? They must recuse themselves and turn it over to the people. It's highly likely that the American people in this case can see further. Yet one more insider, Tea Party activist Dana Loesch, discounts the people.

How to investigate Obama now

World Net Daily again provides a model of how to properly investigate Obama's illegal presidency.

Recently in separate articles WND editor Joseph Farah and columnist Diana West again recommended revisiting Obama's legal qualifications to be president. Intuitively they suggested an official investigation should take place—for the first time.

Recall in 2011 WND published the New York Times bestseller (Corsi's *Where's the Birth Certificate?*) which pressured Obama to immediately produce an alleged complete birth certificate after years of refusing to release it. Reputable forensic document examiners determined it was almost certainly phony.

My own extensive forensic profile decoding of Obama's super-intel showed the same thing after I analyzed Obama's comments. The National Review found Obama's birth certificate unworthy of an investigation or even a mention in the magazine.

America's primary printed voice of conservatism simply shrugged.

7

FROM WALL STREET TO THE ATLANTIC,

OBAMA ENABLED, TRUMP ATTACKED

The Wall Street Journal
Bret Stephens
wsj.com/articles/out-clintoning-the-clintons-
1464642622?tesla=y

What did President Obama know and when

Now we come to Wall Street Journal writer Bret Stephens' recent article—one of the most powerful secret confessions of any journalist who unconsciously has been looking straight at an illegal president Obama. Like his colleagues he displaces the deception onto Trump. He tells one formidable super-intel story with persuasive imagery matching Obama's recent confession.

Alluding back to the Watergate hearings, Stephens introduces the one central question for Obama, "What did the president know and when did he know it?" He adds, "The country never got a believable answer from the White House."

Before we go further, appreciate that Stephens quickly holds up the idea of decoding deeper super-intel messages and alludes to the distinct two-level mind: conscious and unconscious. He informs us, "We're all semioticians now, trying to decode the meaning of Donald Trump's doublespeak." To translate "semioticians" he means "I'm communicating unconsciously on a deeper level in a symbolic language—of projection." He's inviting his readers to decode the deeper meaning of his messages about Trump.

As we will see, when he speaks literally of Trump he's symbolically talking about Obama. Stephens' super-intel vividly describes its special language. In essence it declares, "I speak symbolically." One more journalist confesses we should substitute "Obama'" for "Trump" in his story.

Stephens confesses how confused he is consciously and how oblivious he remains to his own "doublespeak"—subconscious communication. Consciously he's blind, unconsciously he sees. But his own doublespeak is the healthy, super-intel form of doublespeak that identifies projections attempting to help a person own the truth, rather than most doubletalk designed to overtly deceive while trying to consciously cover up the truth.

In this particularly vicious article, the writer refers to "picking through the word jumble gushing out of Mr. Trump's [read Obama's] mouth."

First he suggests the super-intel decoding process: "pick through" his own communications in this article to decipher his key unconscious messages and a consistent super-intel story. Deep down he knows that—regarding Obama—this is exactly what his own super intelligence has been doing over the past eight years: reading his numerous communications for deeper messages. He has heard the consistent secret story Obama has been telling, but consciously Stephens has no idea he has picked up on it.

'Doublespeak...nothing new'

Back to Trump, Stephens quickly connects him to the Clintons and then to Obama.

He asserts that *deceptive "doublespeak"* is "nothing new" in politicians. He tells us of the Clintons [also implying Obama] who "pioneered a form of political doublespeak." He suggests a brand new pioneering deception unlike anything in American history has taken place. He then links that to Obama's public opposition to gay marriage until 2012. He adds, "The ordinary voter might have treated the [change of face] as a betrayal." Symbolically he's telling us Obama has been two-faced in his commitment (marriage) to the American people and overtly betrayed them.

Stephens implies he saw plainly in the back of his mind that Obama betrayed the voters when he was elected–and that a revote should be taken now.

To remove all doubt that Stephens is unconsciously referring to Obama's betrayal with an illegal presidency, he takes us to the heart of his story. In another projection onto Trump alluding to Obama, he mentions, "What you won't get is a satisfactory response to the basic question…." He now adds the punch line, "There was a time when there was a price to be paid in American politics for evading questions."

Stephens reminds us that in 1973 regarding the Watergate scandal, Sen. Howard Baker famously asked, "What did the president know and when did he know it?" Stephens writes, "The country never got a believable answer from the White House, and Nixon resigned the presidency the following year."

Remember to decode his symbolic story as you would a parable. Obama betrayed America in a unique way, beginning by hiding his true origin. For years he continually evaded the central question. "What did you know about where you were born and when? What did you know about the legality of your presidency and when? Did you produce a legal birth certificate? Does one actually exist?"

Stephens implies a further confrontation of Obama whose behavior shouts out the obvious answer. He doesn't have a true birth certificate—there's not one in Hawaii. The one he produced is a forgery, and—Stephens' super-intel insists—the country has never gotten a believable answer from Obama or the Democratic Party?

The Wall Street Journal writer agrees with his media colleague, Roger L. Simon. This scandal is so foundation-shattering that it clearly eclipses Watergate.

Birther conspiracy cited

To verify his super-intel observations, Stephens implies that a Senate investigation of Obama's birth certificate should be conducted. He secretly urges some Senate leader to have the courage of Howard Baker and speak out. He's talking about now and another "famous question" that begs to be asked, "Mr. President, are you a legal president?"

The writer then confirms his earth-shaking super-intel message with another huge projection—accusing Trump of birther conspiracy. No doubt Obama's illegal presidency hangs heavily on Stephens' deeper mind.

"If Mrs. Clinton's misstatements about her emails make her unfit for office, what are we to make of the serial and slanderous conspiracy theories that have been Mr. Trump's political stock-in-trade for years?" Stephens reveals just how flippantly he took the question of Obama's potential illegal presidency and how flippantly he took the Constitution.

He confesses just how serial and slanderous was the mocking anti-birther movement, Stephens' personal stock-in-trade for years, his and so many of his media colleagues. His undercover super-intel reporting confirms that the media and the political class recoiled at the thought of challenging Obama, to make him accountable to the Constitution. Stephens is now reporting that something dark, something buried in the deep unconscious, prevented the political class from pursuing that course.

New investigation of journalists

He's opened a whole new area of investigation: why it was so totally unacceptable to investigate Obama's credentials. He follows with another Trump projection confessing in part the unconscious answer he's picked up about himself and his media colleagues. He points to his own guilt and how he didn't care enough to investigate Obama: "Maybe the answer is that Trump's supporters [read Obama' supporters like Stephens] don't care about his lies because… they're participating in a wink-and-nod routine with their candidate."

Hear Stephen's indictment: When Obama was a candidate, the media and the entire Beltway participated in an unconscious "wink-and-nod routine"—a huge cover-up lie. This is the sad state to which America has sunk. We have a foreign-born president, and no court nor press nor Congress to expose and address that illegality.

To reveal how absurd his conscious thinking has become, Stephens equates Trump University lawsuits with the charges against Hillary Clinton for favors she delivered to foreign donors to her Clinton Foundation. Stephens reveals how severely his own guilty conscience condemns him for his failure to investigate Obama's presidency.

Revealing the extent of his blindness, he continues in projection confession mode. "Point out contradictions [to Trump]…he's likely to rejoin that you're a loser who's been wrong about everything and doesn't understand the art of leadership." Stephens suggests his enormous contradictions as a journalist and his own super-intel assessment that he's a loser who has been wrong especially about Obama's cover-up and about Trump's leadership abilities. Trump remains the one man who has confronted Obama and could still lead America to do so.

Stephens repeats the message. Point out Trump contradictions to his admirers and "They'll say you're missing the deeper point…Mr. Trump is reflecting the anger of everyday Americans who want a pragmatist in the White House whose instinct is to put America first and negotiate the details later."

Trump could reveal Obama's true status

In other words, voters are angry at an illegal Obama. He has fueled that anger with his extensive presidential abuse. They now want a practical man in the White House who has seen all along who Obama really is. Obama has never put America first, but Trump can and should negotiate the details of Obama's true status later. The people see that it needs to be done.

Stephens does too but—when it comes to Obama—the writer confesses he has continually failed to put America first. In rich symbolic imagery, his super-intel basically calls him a coward in one more Trump projection, "He lambastes our allies as freeloaders and military nincompoops who throw down their arms at the first sign of danger." Stephens saw that Obama was a freeloader but immediately buried the truth. Instead, he threw down his powerful journalistic arms at the first sign he would have to unpopularly stand up to the anti-birther propaganda. He was compelled to join forces with his mainstream colleagues, all of whom were equally in retreat.

But unconsciously Stephens puts his finger on the one trait America's leaders sorely lacked when it came to Obama—courage. The courage to stand up for the rule of law. Stephens implies that until we do, we will remain in retreat. He's making a powerful super-intel speech if we can hear it. He's speaking passionately to American leaders and himself. Of course we know he's totally closed to his unconscious eyes.

In the end he's particularly pleading with the American people who have already absorbed the same story he has.

But instead of showing the courage to face up to danger, Stephens confesses that he's all about being a bully in a gang of bullies.

Not to say he can't see a fault in Trump, but he's blind to his own bigger fault. In another projection assessment of Trump, Stephens asserts "The words are rubbish; the attacks are pure theater; the promises are negotiable; the facts are an irrelevance. What matters is power: my getting it, you getting out of the way."

Again Stephens unconsciously describes Obama as an illegal president. His words rubbish, his alleged attacks on America's enemies are pure theater, his promises negotiable, fluctuating with the political wind and most of all the facts regarding the legality of his presidency irrelevant. What matters is power for power's sake, don't oppose me—a perfect fit with Obama's mentor, Saul Alinsky, and his controller, radical Islam.

The same imagery applies to Stephens in his hit piece on Trump. It's as though he's saying, "The facts are now irrelevant to me. My words about Trump are rubbish because I'm so busy projecting. My promises to my journalistic duties are negotiable. The facts about Obama are irrelevant." And that's how Stephens treated them.

Stephens degrades Obama doubters

Stephens taps into another powerful motive as to why the media refused to acknowledge Obama's illegality. He wants power, he wants to be consciously right, and he'll bully the truth to do it. It's so bad he would attack the millions of citizens who had serious questions about Obama's legal presidency—labeling them paranoid, conspiratorial and ignorant, all summed up in the degrading name he used for them, "birthers."

Immediately after his "wink-and-nod" reference to enabling an illegal presidency, Stephens concludes with another major self-indictment of his blindness but more.

"We are a country of sophisticated people. We assume that all politicians are liars. We can't be scandalized. Nobody takes us for suckers. We nominate people like Mr. Trump and Mrs. Clinton because we think we see through them and nonetheless like enough of what we see to elect them to the presidency. Maybe we have it wrong. Maybe they're the ones who see through us."

Stephens unconsciously sees through Obama. Consciously he's sophisticated and has a superficial understanding that "all politicians are liars."

Read his Trump projection this way: "We nominate people like Obama [and Hillary Clinton]" and again he's back to Obama's presidential nomination. He saw that Obama could lie but liked him enough to support his election as president. Reading through Stephens' major denials, he confesses that he has been a sucker. He was scandalized by Obama and enabled Obama's lie. Plainly his super-intel reveals: Obama's nomination was a scandal like no other, one that put an illegal president in office. Stephens, the great journalist, was suckered and seduced by Obama, as were millions of Americans.

But deep down he embraced Obama's corruption because secretly he embraced his own as in his earlier phrase "don't care about his lies." In other words, "don't care about my lies." Stephens gives that familiar wink-and-nod to his own mind's ability to lie to himself and his readers.

He has the slightest instinct, "maybe we have it wrong." But the real truth was that he had it so wrong he embraced an illegal presidency—the biggest lie ever associated with an American leader.

He ends with the idea that maybe the corrupt politician sees through us. It's his projection of his super-intel awareness that sees all the way through him.

Stephens offers a powerful explanation for Obama's illegitimate presidency. Obama played on our guilt and our deep innate flawed nature—he lied to us knowing all too many would embrace the lie. If our idealized political heroes lie, we feel better about ourselves—temporarily guilt-free.

Indirectly he also points to Obama's magic calling card— first black president—which enabled him to strongly play on people's guilt. America is not finished working through its racial guilt over past sins, but that takes a long time. Yet the real truth is that racial guilt is at a certain point just a carrier, a representative of deeper guilt.

Note again Stephens' emphasis on right and wrong as in "maybe I'm wrong." Unconsciously "right or wrong" is the central issue deep in his psyche. He wasn't slightly wrong he was off the charts wrong but can't face it consciously.

Trump triggers WSJ guilt

With all his faults, Trump is driving Stephens' guilt-ridden nature—his shadow side—up a wall. That's why the writer he must incessantly berate Trump who had been so right when Stephens was so wrong.

Deep down Stephens confesses he has terribly failed America as a journalist, and the guilt is eating him up. He sees what secretly drives him and his colleagues.

We see how desperate Stephens is to confess—his super-intel soul cannot live with himself. He must confess he was wrong, not right.

Stephens' super-intel moral compass calls for overturning another egregious wrong. Obama or anyone else who broke the rule of law must be held accountable.

In the end, the super-intel invariably presents a natural law moral of the story. Here Stephens underscores our politically correct culture—we're never wrong. And in its beaming self-pride, the politically correct culture will bring down our formerly humble yet great nation.

It all comes down to developing the courage to own our wrongs. The courage to see "right and wrong" exist. Yet we have a problem. In an essay answering the question, "Why did Jesus have to die?" the renowned British scholar and novelist, C. S. Lewis, wrote that "it needs a good man to repent. And here's the catch. Only a bad person needs to repent: only a good person can repent perfectly."

The Atlantic
Portrait of a Presidential Mind
Reflections on Jeffrey Goldberg's interview with President Obama.

http://www.theatlantic.com/magazine/archive/2016/04/portrait-of-a-presidential-mind/471528/

The April 2016 edition of The Atlantic (previously known as The Atlantic Monthly) featured an extensive interview with Obama focusing on foreign policy conducted by American-Israeli journalist Jeffrey Goldberg. In a summary article, writer James Bennet unconsciously picked up on the overriding issue of Obama's illegal presidency.

Immediately Bennet presents the 2016 presidential campaign as a projection template for Obama's 2008 campaign. He notes "this presidential campaign [Obama's in 2008] is presenting fantastical accounts of America's [that is Obama's] power to bend the world to its will"—"even by the comic-book standards of American politics."

Deep down he reports Obama's stolen presidency was a joke, a fantasy in which this illegal leader bent America to his will. Sarcasm aside, Bennet declares America in 2016 with a new president can be "immigrant-free"—that is free of this immigrant president."

He also mentioned how Obama, "so alone…has repeatedly tossed aside…the 'Washington playbook' on foreign affairs." That is, he repeatedly violated the Constitution regarding a foreign citizen becoming a U.S. president.

Now for the punch line. The writer then ridicules Trump's vision of "saintly might" suggesting *"someone remind Donald Trump that Superman was an illegal immigrant."* A clear reference to the 2008 "Superman President" Barack Obama, the illegal White House Messiah. His projection plainly declares without question Obama is an illegal immigrant. Unconsciously the writer strongly advises Trump to pursue the truth about Obama's illegality.

Reporter picks up Obama's confession

Over his eight years in office Obama has continued to unconsciously confess to his illegal presidency. He does so again in his interview with The Atlantic. Unknowingly, Jeffrey Goldberg revealed how clearly his super-intel heard Obama's secret confession reflected in specific Obama comments. Here are brief excerpts.

- He detests "free riders."

- Introduces "the anti-free rider campaign" (confront his illegality).

- Speaks of those irresponsible people who "don't... want to help shoulder the burden...of dealing with urgent global threats" (both his illegal presidency and destructive behavior).

- "We don't have to always be the ones who are up front," (deceitful, leader in retreat).

- He's upset over the accusation of "leading from behind;" (a phony leader confession).

- Likens the entire Middle East to Gotham in the "Batman" comic books, where thugs (other countries) divide up the city but the Joker he identifies as ISIS who burns up the whole city. He insists they must be stopped. Not only is Obama "ISIS" which he enabled to destroy the Middle East, he's also "the Joker" (illegal president) who destroys America with efforts to destroy the entire world (i.e. the Iran deal). His super-intel pleads for the people to stop him, make plain his illegal presidency.
- Obama refers to historians who criticize him for pressing

the "pause button in Syria" when they crossed the red line. "Pause button" implies no authentic leader in office. He knows historians (or journalists) will eventually see that he crossed constitutional "red line" as an illegal immigrant. Obama denies his mistake but knows "my credibility was at stake, that America's credibility was at stake." In other words, the credibility of the rule of law is at stake for America with his illegal presidency.

- As noted above, key reporters scapegoat Trump over their guilt for overlooking Obama's illegality. They displace their 2008 reporting failure onto Trump's 2016 candidacy.

A new fairy tale: The emperor Obama with no birth certificate on

Not only did the national media demonstrate major avoidance regarding the question of Obama's legal presidency, they quickly took the next step in subconsciously protecting him. Once a seemingly authentic "President Obama" took office, they were full-fledged members of the "anti-birther" propaganda team. The first black president simply was above reproach, and all too many simply idealized him, "I'm okay, he's okay, we're all okay."

Many people were induced to drink the Kool-Aid and looked for every reason to keep up his popularity numbers. Denial can do wonders for such polls. His numerous bad decisions and aggravating behavior were simply chalked up to his liberal ideology and his globalist viewpoint.

In short we had a powerful new version of Hans Christian Andersen's popular fairy tale of the emperor with no clothes on that offers us wisdom from history—collective blind spots that function to keep idealized public figures in power.

The current twist of the fairy tale is the emperor Obama with no authentic birth certificate on as the political crowd on both sides of the aisle declare, "Oh, I see his birth certificate on him…I see it too…we all see it. Yes…yes…yes!"

Yet the stunning reality remains that no person in America has seen an independently authenticated birth certificate.

The emperor-with-no-clothes crowd would naively say some state of Hawaii official claimed it was authentic, but that turned out to be nothing but a rumor. Of course Obama implicitly agrees with the rumor as does the media.

The current myth has massive implications for the entire world. Virtually no one can entertain the question, "What would it mean for America if Barack Obama was truly an illegal president?"

Be careful of powerful questions, questions which the media assiduously avoid. But the super-intel has its own totally independent unique view. Independent of conscious-mind political inclinations, the super-intel it has its own popularity poll. And it sees deeper, quicker, faster and always the truth, so help it God who created its strong natural law never-break-not-even-bend moral compass.

Millions of Americans see it and experience his abuse up close and personal. The American people have overwhelmingly declared him as the worst president in U. S. history.

Do you think it's impossible for the forces of deceit that inspire radical Islam to get control of Obama and plant a Stockholm Syndrome U.S. president in office? All it took was one bright mixed-race child, the product of a tumultuous relationship between an American woman and a Kenyan father who despised the West, a man with a background of severe abuse himself who abused women, children and himself.

As president, Obama turned that unending cycle of abuse on America itself, its Constitution and its rule of law. Donald Trump may be the one man capable of forcing the truth to the surface now, so that American can finally heal.

Conclusion

The deepest underlying issue in this election is the illegal presidency of Barack Obama.

Typical of denial, the Democrats displace the guilt by attacking Trump with a vengeance as an unfit candidate—but secretly afraid he will expose Obama's horrific deed. Again Trump remains the one candidate with a documented history of calling Obama out on this issue. The liberal media is obsessed with degrading Trump with "birther" charges— unable to let the matter rest, unconsciously pointing to the media's own culpability in allowing his illegal presidency.

On the Republican side, the "anybody but Trump" people are terrified that he would expose their utter failure to stand up for the Constitution, giving in to a "tulip mania" Obama candidacy. They must scapegoat Trump, insisting on his incompetence and continue to punish themselves by destroying his chances for election. Not only are they destroying their party, they are destroying the country's foundational rule of law and encouraging an Obama clone to continue the liberal destruction of America.

Epilogue

For political expediency on Sept. 16, 2016 Donald Trump renounced his birther position in the face of continued politically correct media protection of Obama. The media and other Obama supporters simply label as racist anyone who insists that he was legally ineligible to be elected president of the United States. They also continue bullying millions of Americans who have serious rule of law questions about Obama's presidency. Yet the guilt-ridden media cannot stop introducing the birther issue. Why? Their super intelligence tells them Obama has consistently disregarded the Constitution and the rule of law which inspired it. And the media carries a deep-seated guilt for having enabled this illegal president whose own background of abuse has made him a puppet to the terrorist Islamic state.

Acknowledgements

I'm indebted to two fine editors, Russ Tarby and Duncan Jaenicke, who saw this book through to completion. Ellen Sallas also provided great help with her creative book-production skills. My agent, Greg Johnson of WordServe Literary Group and FaithHappenings.com, was a steady source of counsel. My website designer, Carlton Smith of Flagstone Search Marketing, was invaluable with his experience and marketing plans.

Also a special thanks goes to Mike Klassen, director of World Ahead Press the co-publishing division of WND Books. He offered timely suggestions after discussing the project with me.

About the Author

ANDREW G. HODGES, M.D., is a psychiatrist in private practice. He previously served as an assistant clinical professor of psychiatry at the University of Alabama at Birmingham School of Medicine. Dr. Hodges has helped pioneer a breakthrough to the brilliant unconscious mind, which he explained in his 1994 groundbreaking book *The Deeper Intelligence* (which he now calls the "super intelligence"). The newly discovered unconscious operates hundreds of times faster than the conscious mind. It sees the whole truth including consciously overlooked motives.

A noted forensic profiler, Hodges developed his "thoughtprint decoding" technique by uniquely accessing unconscious super intelligence messages of suspects during criminal investigations. He bases his analyses on forensic documents—verbatim testimony, transcripts of police interrogations, letters and emails created by the suspects.

Dr. Hodges discovered a deeper moral compass which prompts people to invariably tell the truth—between the lines—in the special symbolic "thoughtprint" language of the subconscious. Tracing repeat matching "thoughtprints" — unique in each case— verifies the message. His work has added an entirely new dimension to the science of psycholinguistics.

Law-enforcement authorities nationwide, including the FBI, have consulted him. Criminal investigators and journalists have sought Hodges' expertise on cases ranging from the murder of JonBenét Ramsey in 1996 to the high-profile disappearance of Natalee Holloway in 2005. In the Ramsey case he applied his technique to the infamous ransom note then wrote two highly acclaimed books on the case, *A Mother Gone Bad* and *Who Will Speak for JonBenét?* (Village

124

House, 1998 and 2000).

He also collaborated with the former police chief of the Wichita Police Department in 2005, just weeks before the apprehension of the "BTK killer." Hodges was the only expert to accurately predict that BTK would kill again after 20 years of dormancy, as the perpetrator later confessed.

In the Natalee Holloway case, Hodges described the exact scenario to which Joran van der Sloot confessed in conversations secretly videotaped months after Hodges' prediction. The FBI consulted with Hodges at the request of Aruban authorities who read his profile. His book, *Into the Deep: The Hidden Confession of Natalee's Killer* (Village House, 2007), told the whole story.

Next in the Amanda Knox case, Hodges examined her revealing email written right after the 2007 murder of her college roommate in Perugia, Italy. Between the lines she confessed to the murder disclosing her motives, her method and her accomplices—confirmed in multiple other jail writings at the time and a major book. Hodges described the whole saga in his book, *As Done Unto You: The Secret Confession of Amanda Knox (Village House, 2015)*.

He also has written for a major FBI publication and presented his cutting-edge technique at a law-enforcement conference at the FBI training facility in Quantico, Virginia.

In other writings he has shown how super-intel communication helps in understanding leaders and in providing a deeper moral compass to address social issues. He utilized decoding techniques to explore the human personality of Jesus Christ in his book, *Jesus: An Interview Across Time— A Psychiatrist Looks at His Humanity* (Bantam, 1988), which religion columnist Mike McManus called "the most important book I've read besides the Bible." Also Hodges' book told the courageous story of his father's lifesaving WW II exploits, *Behind Nazi Lines: My Father's Heroic Quest to Save 149 World War II POWs* (Berkley Books, 2015).

The author has been interviewed extensively in the media with appearances on Fox News, *Geraldo at Large, Hannity,* CNN's *Anderson Cooper 360,* ABC's *The View,* and Court TV.

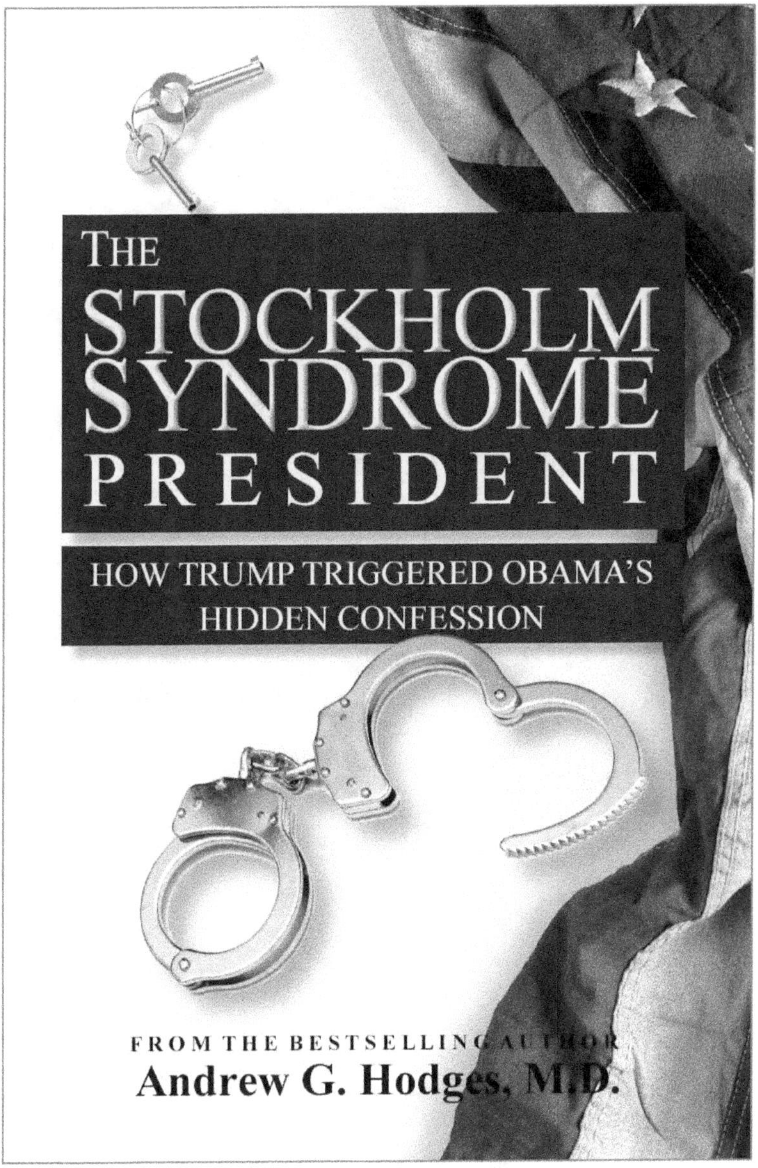

THE
STOCKHOLM SYNDROME
PRESIDENT

HOW TRUMP TRIGGERED OBAMA'S HIDDEN CONFESSION

FROM THE BESTSELLING AUTHOR
Andrew G. Hodges, M.D.

Village House Publishers